# From the Source:

## *Readings in*

# Economics and Government

## *with Answer Key*

**HOLT, RINEHART AND WINSTON**

*Harcourt Brace & Company*

**Austin** • New York • Orlando • Atlanta • San Francisco • Boston • Dallas • Toronto • London

ISBN 0-03-052519-5

15 16 17 18  095  09 08 07 06

# CONTENTS

## PRIMARY SOURCE READINGS

*From the Source: Readings in Economics and Government with Answer Key* provides a comprehensive collection of primary source materials designed to supplement teacher instruction in the areas of economics and government. To enhance this booklet's ease of use, the 73 readings contained in the booklet have been organized into four categories: historical documents, speeches, legal statutes, and primary source readings. By using the readings in this booklet, students will be able to broaden their base of sources of information about economics and government.

Overall, the readings provide a range of historical and contemporary primary source material that varies in style, tone, and level of difficulty. Excerpts from classic sources, such as the Mayflower Compact, George Washington's Farewell Address, and Adam Smith's *The Wealth of Nations*, are included, as well as excerpts from such contemporary sources as the Americans with Disabilities Act and the *Contract with America*. Teachers will find that the readings can be applied to a broad range of concepts, ideas, and topics in the areas of economics and government.

All readings in *From the Source: Readings in Economics and Government with Answer Key* reflect the following general format.

- **Introduction** Each reading begins with a short introduction that provides a context for the upcoming excerpt. This section provides background information about the reading, ties the reading to a concept, idea, or topic in economics or government, and, as appropriate, gives some information about the writer or writers.

- **Excerpt** With the exception of Reading 7: Articles of Confederation, which is four pages long, all readings in *From the Source: Readings in Economics and Government with Answer Key* are either one or two pages in length. Teachers will find that the manageable length of the readings makes them ideal for a variety of applications such as classroom assignments, group discussions, or homework assignments. To facilitate the clarity and usefulness of the readings, bracketed definitions of difficult or obscure terms have been added at point of use.

- **Thinking Critically** The final element in each reading consists of questions that require students to consider and analyze what they have read, draw conclusions, state and defend a point of view, synthesize information, or formulate generalizations based on the knowledge gained from their reading. Sample answers begin on page 113 of this booklet.

Whether the readings are used to supplement classroom instruction, as homework assignments, or as extra-credit assignments, you may wish to give students the opportunity to discuss the readings in small groups or as a class. Have students relate the readings to other information they have acquired about the same topics. You may also wish to give students the opportunity to practice their writing skills by having them write reaction papers to selected readings.

# Magna Carta

In 1215 an assembly of English nobles confronted an oppressive King John and forced him to sign Magna Carta, or Great Charter. Magna Carta limited the power of the king and made it clear that even the king was not above the law. It also contained such ideas as trial by a jury of one's peers and the guarantee of protection against loss of life, liberty, and property, except in accordance with proper legal procedures. Although the concepts contained in Magna Carta originally applied only to nobles, they eventually spread to all English citizens. And nearly 600 years after it was written, Magna Carta was to serve as an inspiration for the American independence movement.

John, by the grace of God, King of England, Lord of Ireland, Duke of Normandy and Aquitaine, and Earl of Anjou: to his archbishops, bishops, abbots, earls, barons, justiciaries [royal judiciary officers], foresters, sheriffs, governors, officers, and to all bailiffs [sheriff's deputies], and his faithful subjects—Greeting.

Know ye, that we, in the presence of God, . . . have confirmed [given assurance], for us and our heirs forever:

1. That the English Church shall be free, and shall have her whole rights and her liberties inviolable [safe from sudden change]. . . .

We have also granted to all the freemen of our kingdom, for us and our heirs forever, all the underwritten liberties, to be enjoyed and held by them and by their heirs, from us and from our heirs. . . .

12. No scutage [tax for military purposes] nor aid shall be imposed in our kingdom, unless by the common council of our kingdom. . . .

14. And also to have the common council of the kingdom, we will cause to be summoned the archbishops, bishops, abbots, earls, and great barons, individually by our letters. . . .

38. No bailiff, for the future, shall put any man to his law upon his own simple affirmation, without credible witnesses produced for that purpose.

39. No freeman shall be seized, imprisoned, dispossessed [deprived of land], outlawed, or exiled, or in any way destroyed; nor will we proceed against or prosecute him except by the lawful judgment of his peers, or by the law of the land.

40. To none will we sell, to none will we deny, to none will we delay right or justice.

41. All merchants shall have safety and security in coming into England, and going out of England, and in staying in and traveling through England, as well by land as by water to buy and sell, without any unjust exactions [demands], according to ancient and right customs, excepting in the time of war, and if they be of a country at war against us . . . they shall be apprehended without injury . . . until it be known to us or to our Chief Justiciary how the merchants of our country are treated who are found in the country at war against us; and if ours be in safety there, the others shall be in safety in our land.

42. It shall be lawful to any person, for the future, to go out of our kingdom, and to return, safely and securely by land or by water, saving [preserving] his allegiance to us, unless it be in time of war, for some short space, for the common good of the kingdom. . . .

60. Also all these customs and liberties aforesaid, which we have granted to be held in our kingdom, for so much of it as belongs to us, all our subjects, as well clergy as laity [nonclergy, or laymen], shall observe toward their tenants as far as concerns them. . . .

63. Wherefore our will is, and we firmly command that the Church of England be free, and that the men in our kingdom have and hold the aforesaid liberties, rights, and concessions, well and in peace, freely and quietly, fully and entirely, to them and their heirs, of us and our heirs, in all things and places forever, as is aforesaid. It is also

sworn, both on our part and on that of the barons, that all the aforesaid should be observed in good faith and without any evil intention. . . .

Given by our hand in the meadow which is called Runnymede, between Windsor and Staines, this 15th day of June, in the 17th year of our reign.

≈≈≈≈≈≈≈≈≈≈≈≈≈≈≈≈≈≈≈≈≈≈≈≈≈≈≈≈≈≈≈≈≈≈≈

## THINKING CRITICALLY

1. What elements of this document are similar to the principles of the U.S. legal system?
2. In what instances did the government reserve the right to suppress a person's freedom of movement?
3. How does the content of this document relate to the demands made by American colonists in their fight for independence?

# Mayflower Compact

In September 1620 a group of 102 men, women, and children, known as Pilgrims, set sail aboard the *Mayflower* in the hope of establishing a new life for themselves in Virginia—a life free from religious persecution. The ship was blown far off course, however, and in November finally anchored off the shore of Massachusetts' Cape Cod Bay. Having no charter to settle in New England and therefore no legal government, Pilgrim leaders drew up a plan by which to maintain order in their new colony and asked all 41 men aboard the *Mayflower* to sign it. The agreement, known as the Mayflower Compact, remained in effect until the Pilgrims' colony was absorbed into that of the Massachusetts Bay in 1691. The Mayflower Compact represented one of the first forms of self-government in North America, one based on the consent of the governed.

We whose names are underwritten, the loyal subjects of our dread sovereign lord, King James, by the grace of God, of Great Britain, France, and Ireland, King, Defender of the Faith, etc.

Having undertaken, for the glory of God, and advancement of the Christian faith and honor of our king and country, a voyage to plant the first colony in the northern parts of Virginia, do by these present, solemnly and mutually, in the presence of God and one of another, covenant [solemnly agree] and combine ourselves together into a civil body politic, for our better ordering and preservation and furtherance of the ends aforesaid; and by virtue hereof to enact, constitute, and frame such just and equal laws, ordinances, acts, constitutions, offices from time to time as shall be thought most meet and convenient for the general good of the colony; unto which we promise all due submission and obedience. In witness whereof we have hereunder subscribed our names, Cape Cod, 11th of November, in the year of the reign of our sovereign lord, King James, of England, France, and Ireland 18, and of Scotland 54. Anno Domini 1620.

## THINKING CRITICALLY

1. According to the Compact, why did the Pilgrims make their voyage?
2. Why did the Pilgrims sign the Compact?
3. Do you think it was necessary for the Pilgrims to sign such an agreement? Why or why not?

# English Petition of Right

Arbitrary and unlawful actions of the English kings of the 1600s led the English Parliament in 1628 to draft the following statement of grievances. The document, which was presented by Parliament to King Charles I and which he accepted, forced the king to make concessions of reform. The ideas contained within the document, particularly the protection of individual freedoms and the principle of taxation only with the consent of the legislature, influenced the political thinking of many American colonists. The right to petition, guaranteed in the First Amendment of the U.S. Bill of Rights, can in part be traced to the English Petition of Right.

### I.

. . . Whereas, It is declared and enacted . . . that no tallage [tax] or aid should be laid or levied by the king or his heirs in this realm without the goodwill and assent of the archbishops, bishops, earls, barons, knights, burgesses, and . . . the freemen of the commonalty [the common people] of this realm; and by authority of the Parliament . . . it is declared and enacted that from thenceforth no person . . . [shall] be compelled to make any loans to the king against his will,

### II.

Yet, nevertheless . . . your people have been . . . required to lend certain sums of money to your Majesty; . . .

### III.

And whereas also, By the statute called the Great Charter of the Liberties of England, it is declared and enacted that no freeman may be taken or imprisoned, . . . or be outlawed or exiled or in any manner destroyed, but by the lawful judgment of his peers or by the law of the land.

### IV.

And . . . it was declared and enacted by authority of Parliament that no man . . . should be put out of his land . . . nor imprisoned, nor disinherited, nor put to death, without being brought to answer by due process of law.

### V.

Nevertheless . . . divers [several] of your subjects have of late been imprisoned without any cause showed; . . .

### VI.

And whereas . . . great companies of soldiers and mariners [sailors] have been dispersed into divers counties of the realm, and the inhabitants against their wills have been compelled to receive them into their houses. . . .

### VII.

And whereas also . . . it is declared and enacted that no man should be forejudged of life or limb against the form of the Great Charter and the law of the land; . . . nevertheless of late divers commissions . . . have issued forth, by which certain persons have been assigned and appointed commissioners, with power and authority to proceed within the land according to the justice of martial law [law carried out by military authority]. . . .

### VIII.

By pretext whereof some of your Majesty's subjects have been by some of the said commissioners put to death. . . .

### IX.

Upon pretense that the said offenders were punishable only by martial law . . . which commissions . . . are wholly and directly contrary to the said laws and statutes of this your realm:

### X.

They [your subjects] do therefore humbly pray your most excellent Majesty that no man hereafter be compelled to make or yield any gift, loan, benevolence [special tax levied by English kings for their own benefit], tax, or such like charge without common consent by act of Parliament; and that none be called to make answer, or take such oath, or give attendance, or be confined, or otherwise molested . . . concerning the same, or for refusal thereof; and that no freeman . . . be imprisoned or detained; and that your Majesty would be pleased to remove the said soldiers and mariners; and that your people may not be burdened in time to come; and that the aforesaid commissions for proceeding by martial law may be revoked and annulled; and that hereafter no commissions of like nature may issue forth. . . .

## XI.

. . . and that your Majesty would be also graciously pleased, for the further comfort and safety of your people, to declare your royal will and pleasure that in the things aforesaid all your officers and ministers shall serve you according to the laws and statutes of this realm, as they tender [work for] the honor of your Majesty and the prosperity of this kingdom.

## THINKING CRITICALLY

1. What complaint does the English Parliament make to the king in regard to taxation?

2. What type of law is Parliament protesting?

3. What does the right of petition allow citizens to do? Why is the right of petition important?

# First Charter of Massachusetts

In 1629 the Puritan directors of the Massachusetts Bay Company took their company charter and 1,000 settlers to America, ending their journey in what is now Boston. Maintaining their charter from the beginning made it almost impossible for company investors remaining in England to infringe on the company's control. Having the charter in the colony also generated a sense of independence from English rule among the Massachusetts colonists.

Whereas our most dear and royal father, King James . . . has given and granted unto the Council established at Plymouth, in the County of Devon, for the planting, ruling, ordering, and governing of New England in America, and to their successors and assigns [persons to whom a right is legally transferred] forever, all that part of America lying and being in breadth from 40° north latitude . . . to 48° of the said north latitude, inclusive and in length of and within all the breadth aforesaid throughout the mainlands from sea to sea . . . provided always that the said islands or any the premises by the said letters patent intended and meant to be granted were not then actually possessed or inhabited by any other Christian prince or state. . . .

And . . . to the end that the affairs and businesses which, from time to time, shall happen and arise concerning the said lands and the plantation of the same may be the better managed and ordered, We have further . . . granted and confirmed . . . unto Our said trusty and well-beloved subjects . . . and all such others as shall hereafter be admitted and made free of the Company and Society hereafter mentioned, shall, from time to time and at all times forever hereafter be . . . one body corporate and politic in fact and name . . . and that they and their successors shall and may be capable and enabled as well as to implead [sue or prosecute at law] and to be impleaded, and to prosecute, demand, and answer and be answered unto in all and singular suits, causes, quarrels, and actions of what kind or nature soever. . . .

And Our will and pleasure is . . . that from henceforth forever there shall be one governor, one deputy governor, and eighteen assistants of the said Company, to be from time to time constituted, elected, and chosen out of the freemen of the said Company, for the time being, in such manner and form as hereinafter . . . is expressed, which said officers shall apply themselves to take care for the best disposing and ordering of the general business and affairs of, for, and concerning the said lands and premises . . . and the government of the people there. . . .

And further, We will . . . that the governor of the said Company, for the time being, or in his absence by occasion of sickness or otherwise, the deputy governor, for the time being, shall have authority . . . to give order for the assembling of the said Company and calling them together to consult and advise of the business and affairs of the said Company and . . . shall or may, once every month, or oftener, at their pleasures, assemble and hold and keep a court or assembly of themselves for the better ordering and directing of their affairs. . . . [The] governor or deputy governor and six of the assistants . . . shall have full power and authority to choose, nominate, and appoint such and so many others as they shall fit, and that shall be willing to accept the same, to be free of the said Company and body, and them into the same to admit; and to elect and constitute such officers as they shall think fit and requisite [needed] for the ordering, managing, and dispatching of the affairs of the said governor and Company . . . and to make laws and ordinances for the good and welfare of the said Company . . . and the people inhabiting and to inhabit the same . . . so as such laws and ordinances be not contrary or repugnant to the laws and statutes of this Our Realm of England.

And, further, Our will and pleasure is . . . that all and every the subjects of Us . . . which shall go to and inhabit within the said lands and premises hereby mentioned to be granted and every of their children which shall happen to be born there, or on the seas in going thither or returning from thence, shall have and enjoy all liberties and immunities of free and natural subjects within any of the dominions of Us.

And We do . . . grant . . . that it shall and may be lawful to and for the governor or deputy governor, to make, ordain, and establish all manner of wholesome and reasonable orders, laws, statutes, and ordinances, directions, and instructions not contrary to the laws of this Our Realm of England.

## THINKING CRITICALLY

1. Identify the composition of the government that was to be established by the charter.

2. According to the charter, how were new government officials to come to office?

3. Why do you think the presence of the charter in the colony gave the Massachusetts colonists a sense of independence from English rule?

# Fundamental Orders
# of Connecticut

In 1636 a group of settlers established a colony in the farmlands of the Connecticut River Valley. Recent authoritarian rule in England prompted the settlers to establish a detailed plan of government. The resulting Fundamental Orders of Connecticut, which some regard as the first written constitution in the American colonies, was a step toward modern democracy.

We the inhabitants and residents of Windsor, Hartford, and Wethersfield . . . knowing where a people are gathered together the word of God requires that to maintain the peace and union of such a people there should be an orderly and decent government established according to God . . . therefore associate . . . ourselves to be as one public state or commonwealth; and do, for ourselves and our successors . . . enter into combination and confederation [union] together, to maintain and preserve the liberty and purity of the gospel of our Lord, Jesus, which we now profess . . . and also in our civil affairs to be guided and governed according to such laws, rules, orders, and decrees as shall be made, ordered, and decreed, as follows:

1. It is ordered . . . that there shall be yearly two general assemblies or courts. . . . The first shall be called the Court of Election, wherein shall be yearly chosen . . . so many magistrates and other public officers . . . which . . . shall have power to administer justice according to the laws here established . . . which choice shall be made by all that are admitted freemen and have taken the oath of fidelity [loyalty]. . . .

4. It is ordered . . . that no person be chosen governor above [more than] once in two years, and that the governor be always a member of some approved congregation, and formerly of the magistracy within this jurisdiction; and all the magistrates freemen of this commonwealth. . . .

5. It is ordered . . . that to the aforesaid Court of Election the several towns shall send their deputies, and when the elections are ended they may proceed in any public service as at other courts. Also the other General Court in September

shall be for making of laws; and other public occasion [business], which concerns the good of the commonwealth. . . .

7. It is ordered . . . that after there are warrants given out for any of the said general courts, the constable . . . of each town shall forthwith give notice distinctly to the inhabitants of the same . . . that at a place and time by him or them limited and set, they meet and assemble . . . to elect and choose certain deputies to be at the General Court then following to agitate [discuss in public] the affairs of the commonwealth; . . . deputies shall be chosen by all that are admitted inhabitants in the several towns and have taken the oath of fidelity [loyalty]; provided that none be chosen a deputy for any general court who is not a freeman of this commonwealth. . . .

8. It is ordered . . . that Windsor, Hartford, and Wethersfield shall have power, each town . . . to send four of their freemen as their deputies to every general court; and whatsoever other towns shall be hereafter added to this jurisdiction . . . shall send so many deputies as the court shall judge meet. . . .

9. It is ordered . . . that the deputies thus chosen shall have power and liberty to appoint a time and a place of meeting to gather before any general court to advise and consult of all such things as may concern the good of the public, as also to examine their own elections. . . .

10. It is ordered . . . that [in] every general court . . . shall consist [exist] the supreme power of the commonwealth, and they only shall have power to make laws or repeal them, to grant levies, to admit . . . freemen, dispose of lands undisposed of to several towns or persons, and . . . shall have power to call either court or magistrate or any other

person whatsoever into question for any misdemeanor [wrongdoing], and may for just causes displace [remove from office] or deal otherwise according to the nature of the offense; and . . . may deal . . . [with] any other matter that concerns the good of this commonwealth, except election of magistrates, which shall be done by the whole body of freemen. . . .

11. It is ordered . . . that when any general court . . . has agreed upon any . . . sums of money to be levied upon the several towns within this jurisdiction . . . a committee be chosen to set out and appoint what shall be the proportion of every town to pay of the said levy, provided the committees be made up of an equal number out of each town.

≈≈≈≈≈≈≈≈≈≈≈≈≈≈≈≈≈≈≈≈≈≈≈≈≈≈≈≈≈≈≈≈≈≈≈≈

## THINKING CRITICALLY

1. According to the Fundamental Orders, why did the people of Connecticut establish a commonwealth?

2. What does the Fundamental Orders say in regard to taxation?

3. How is this document different from the Mayflower Compact? Why is the Fundamental Orders considered by some to be the first constitution in the colonies?

# English Bill of Rights

In 1689 the English people drove King James II from the throne. In an attempt to secure the supremacy of the English Parliament in government affairs, members of Parliament drafted and adopted the following Bill of Rights. Many of the rights and freedoms contained in this document were later incorporated into the Constitution of the United States and the American Bill of Rights.

Whereas, the late King James II . . . did endeavor to subvert [overthrow] and extirpate [wipe out] the Protestant religion and the laws and liberties of this kingdom . . . and whereas the said late King James II having abdicated [given up] the government . . . the said Lords . . . being now assembled in a full and free representative of this nation . . . declare:

1. *That* the pretended power of suspending of laws or the execution of laws by regal authority without consent of Parliament is illegal. . . .

3. *That* the commission [authority] for erecting the late [recent] court of commissioners for ecclesiastical causes and all other commissions and courts of like nature are illegal and pernicious [corrupt]. . . .

4. *That* levying money for or to the use of the crown . . . without grant of Parliament . . . is illegal;

5. *That* it is the right of the subjects to petition the king. . . .

6. *That* . . . raising or keeping a standing army within the kingdom in time of peace, unless it be with consent of Parliament, is against law. . . .

8. *That* election of members of Parliament ought to be free;

9. *That* the . . . proceedings in Parliament ought not to be impeached or questioned in any court or place out of Parliament;

10. *That* excessive bail ought not to be required, nor excessive fines imposed, nor cruel and unusual punishments inflicted.

11. *That* jurors ought to be duly impaneled [put on jury duty]. . . .

13. *And that*, for redress [remedy] of all grievances and for the amending, strengthening, and preserving of the laws, Parliaments ought to be held frequently.

## THINKING CRITICALLY

1. According to the Bill of Rights, what offense did King James commit that motivated the people to write this declaration?

2. How does the Bill of Rights ensure that the people will have a voice in their government?

3. What aspects of this document identify the fact that the English government is not a pure democracy?

# Articles of Confederation

On July 12, 1776, a plan to form a confederacy among the 13 states of North America was presented to Congress. The original plan, drafted by John Dickinson of Pennsylvania and agreed upon by a committee made up of one person from each of the states, was much debated by Congress and did not appear in its final form until November 1777. The Articles of Confederation was then ratified by all the states and finally went into effect in 1781.

Articles of Confederation and Perpetual Union Between the States of New Hampshire, Massachusetts Bay, Rhode Island and Providence Plantations, Connecticut, New York, New Jersey, Pennsylvania, Delaware, Maryland, Virginia, North Carolina, South Carolina, and Georgia.

### Article I

The style of this confederacy shall be "The United States of America."

### Article II

Each state retains its sovereignty, freedom, and independence, and every power, jurisdiction, and right which is not by this confederation expressly delegated to the United States in Congress assembled.

### Article III

The said states hereby severally [each by itself] enter into a firm league of friendship with each other, for their common defense, the security of their liberties, and their mutual and general welfare, binding themselves to assist each other against all force offered to, or attacks made upon them, or any of them, on account of religion, sovereignty, trade, or any other pretense whatever.

### Article IV

The better to secure and perpetuate mutual friendship and intercourse [dealings] among the people of the different states in this union, the free inhabitants of each of these states, paupers, vagabonds, and fugitives from justice excepted, shall be entitled to all privileges and immunities of free citizens in the several states; and the people of each state shall have free ingress and regress [entrance and exit] to and from any other state and shall enjoy therein all the privileges of trade and commerce, subject to the same duties, impositions [requirements], and restrictions as the inhabitants thereof respectively. . . .

If any person guilty of or charged with treason, felony, or other high misdemeanor in any state shall flee from justice, and be found in any of the United States, he shall, upon demand of the governor or executive power of the state from which he fled, be delivered up and removed to the state having jurisdiction of his offense.

Full faith and credit shall be given in each of these states to the records, acts, and judicial proceedings of the courts and magistrates of every other state.

### Article V

For the more convenient management of the general interests of the United States, delegates shall be annually appointed in such manner as the legislature of each state shall direct, to meet in Congress. . . .

In determining questions in the United States in Congress assembled, each state shall have one vote.

Freedom of speech and debate in Congress shall not be impeached or questioned in any court or place out of Congress, and the members of Congress shall be protected in their persons from arrests and imprisonments during the time of their going to and from, and attendance on, Congress, except for treason, felony, or breach of the peace.

### Article VI

No state, without the consent of the United States in Congress assembled, shall send any embassy to, or receive any embassy from, or enter into any conference, agreement, alliance, or treaty with any king, prince, or state; nor shall any person holding any office of profit or trust under the United States, or any of them, accept of any present, emolument [payment], office, or title of any kind whatever from any king, prince, or foreign state; nor shall the United States in Congress assembled, or any of them, grant any title of nobility.

No two or more states shall enter into any treaty, confederation, or alliance whatever between them, without the consent of the United States in Congress assembled, specifying accurately the purposes for which the same is to be entered into and how long it shall continue. . . .

No vessels of war shall be kept up in time of peace by any state except such number only as shall be deemed necessary by the United States in Congress assembled for the defense of such state or its trade; nor shall any body of forces be kept up by any state in time of peace except such number only as in the judgment of the United States in Congress assembled shall be deemed requisite to garrison the forts necessary for the defense of said state; but every state shall always keep up a well regulated and disciplined militia, sufficiently armed and accoutered [equipped], and shall provide and constantly have ready for use, in public stores, a due number of field pieces and tents and a proper quantity of arms, ammunition and camp equipage.

No state shall engage in any war without the consent of the United States in Congress assembled unless such state be actually invaded by enemies, or shall have received certain advice of a resolution being formed by some nation of Indians to invade such state, and the danger is so imminent as not to admit of a delay till the United States in Congress assembled can be consulted. . . .

### Article VIII

All charges of war and all other expenses that shall be incurred for the common defense or general welfare, and allowed by the United States in Congress assembled, shall be defrayed [paid] out of a common treasury, which shall be supplied by the several states in proportion to the value of all land within each state, granted to or surveyed for any person, as such land the buildings and improvements thereon shall be estimated according to such mode as the United States in Congress assembled shall from time to time direct and appoint. The taxes for paying that proportion shall be laid and levied by the authority and direction of the legislatures of the several states within the time agreed upon by the United States in Congress assembled.

### Article IX

The United States in Congress assembled shall have the sole and exclusive right and power of determining on peace and war, except in the cases mentioned in the sixth article—of sending and receiving ambassadors—entering into treaties and alliances, provided that no treaty of commerce shall be made whereby the legislative power of the respective states shall be restrained from imposing such imposts and duties on foreigners as their own people are subjected to or from prohibiting the exportation or importation of any species of goods or commodities whatsoever—of establishing rules for deciding in all cases what captures on land or water shall be legal, and in what manner prizes taken by land or naval forces in the service of the United States shall be divided or appropriated—of granting letters of marque and reprisal [retaliating] in times of peace—appointing courts for the trial of piracies and felonies committed on the high seas and establishing courts for receiving and determining finally appeals in all cases of captures, provided that no member of Congress shall be appointed a judge of any of the said courts.

The United States in Congress assembled shall also be the last resort on appeal in all disputes and difference now subsisting or that hereafter may arise between two or more states concerning boundary, jurisdiction, or any other cause whatever, which authority shall always be exercised in the manner following: Whenever the legislative or executive authority or lawful agent of any state in controversy with another shall present a petition to Congress stating the matter in question and praying for a hearing, notice thereof shall be given by order of Congress to the legislative or executive authority of the other state in controversy, and a day assigned for the appearance of the parties by their lawful agents, who shall then be directed to appoint, by joint consent, commissioners or judges to constitute a court for hearing and determining the matter in question. . . .

If any of the parties shall refuse to submit to the authority of such court, or to appear or defend their claim or cause, the court shall nevertheless proceed to pronounce sentence or judgment, which shall in like manner be final and decisive, the judgment or sentence and other proceedings being in either case transmitted to Congress and lodged among the acts of Congress for the security of the parties concerned. Provided that every commissioner, before he sits in judgment, shall take an oath to be administered by one of the judges of the supreme or superior court of the state where the cause shall be tried, "well and truly to hear and determine the matter in question, according to the best of his judgment, without favor, affection, or hope of reward": provided, also, that no state shall be deprived of territory for the benefit of the United States. . . .

The United States in Congress assembled shall also have the sole and exclusive right and power of regulating the alloy and value of coin struck by their own authority or by that of the respective states—fixing the standard of weights and measures throughout the United States—regulating the trade and managing all affairs with the Indians not members of any of the states, provided that the legislative right of any state within its own limits be not infringed or violated—establishing or regulating post offices from one state to another, throughout all the United States, and exacting such postage on the papers passing through the same as may be requisite to defray the expenses of the said office—appointing all officers of the land forces in the service of the United States excepting regimental officers—appointing all the officers of the naval forces, and commissioning all officers whatever in the service of the United States—making rules for the government and regulation of the said land and naval forces, and directing their operations. . . .

The United States in Congress assembled shall never engage in a war, nor grant letters of marque and reprisal in time of peace, nor enter into any treaties or alliances, nor coin money, nor regulate the value thereof, nor ascertain the sums and expenses necessary for the defense and welfare of the United States, or any of them, nor emit bills, nor borrow money on the credit of the United States, nor appropriate money, nor agree upon the number of vessels of war to be built or purchased or the number of land or sea forces to be raised, nor appoint a commander in chief of the Army or Navy, unless nine states assent [agree] to the same; nor shall a question on any other point, except for

adjourning from day to day, be determined unless by the votes of a majority of the United States in Congress assembled.

The Congress of the United States shall have power to adjourn to any time within the year, and to any place within the United States, so that no period of adjournment be for a longer duration than the space of six months, and shall publish the journal of their proceedings monthly, except such parts thereof relating to treaties, alliances, or military operations as in their judgment require secrecy; and the yeas and nays of the delegates of each state on any question shall be entered on the journal when it is desired by any delegate, and the delegates of a state, or any of them, at his or their request, shall be furnished with a transcript of the said journal, except such parts as are above excepted, to lay before the legislatures of the several states.

### Article X

The Committee of the States, or any nine of them, shall be authorized to execute, in [during] the recess of Congress, such of the powers of Congress as the United States in Congress assembled, by the consent of nine states, shall from time to time think expedient [appropriate] to vest them with [give them]; provided that no power be delegated to the said committee, for the exercise of which, by the Articles of Confederation, the voice of nine states in the Congress of the United States assembled is requisite [required].

### Article XI

Canada acceding [agreeing] to this Confederation, and joining in the measures of the United States, shall be admitted into and entitled to all the advantages of this union; but no other colony shall be admitted into the same unless such admission be agreed to by nine states.

### Article XII

All bills of credit emitted, moneys borrowed, and debts contracted by or under the authority of Congress, before the assembling of the United States, in pursuance [a carrying out] of the present Confederation, shall be deemed and considered as a charge against the United States, for payment and satisfaction whereof the said United States and the public faith are hereby solemnly pledged.

### Article XIII

Every state shall abide by the determinations of the United States in Congress assembled on all questions which by this Confederation are submitted to them. And the Articles of this Confederation shall be inviolably [wholly] observed by every state, and the union shall be perpetual; nor shall any alteration at any time hereafter be made in any of them; unless such alteration be agreed to in a Congress of the United States and be afterward confirmed by the legislatures of every state.

And whereas it has pleased the Great Governor of the world to incline the hearts of the legislatures we respectively represent in Congress to approve of, and to authorize us to ratify the said Articles of Confederation and Perpetual Union. Know ye that we the undersigned delegates, by virtue of the power and authority to us given for that purpose, do by these presents, in the name and in behalf of our respective constituents [citizens represented by the delegates], fully and entirely ratify and confirm each and every of the said Articles of Confederation and Perpetual Union and all and singular [each and every one of] the matters and things therein contained. And we do further solemnly plight [pledge] and engage the faith of our respective constituents that they shall abide by [accept without objection] the determinations of the United States in Congress assembled on all questions which by the said Confederation are submitted to them. And that the articles thereof shall be inviolably observed by the states we respectively represent, and that the union shall be perpetual. In witness whereof we have hereunto set our hands in Congress.

## THINKING CRITICALLY

1. What is the stated purpose of the confederation?
2. How were members of Congress to be chosen?
3. What provisions did the Articles of Confederation make to ensure that a monarchy would not be established in the United States?
4. Under what circumstances could a state engage in war without the consent of Congress?
5. How was the new government to be financed?
6. What do the Articles say in regard to any state being denied its territory for the benefit of the nation?
7. Who has the power to monitor the postal system?
8. How many states must consent before Congress can execute most of its powers, i.e., the power to wage war?
9. What provisions are made to ensure that the states know of the activities and votes of Congress?
10. To whom was the opportunity to join the union offered?
11. What happened to debts previously acquired by the United States?
12. In your opinion, was this "firm league of friendship" sufficient to hold the United States together as a nation? Why or why not?

# Declaration of the Rights of Man and Citizen

The Declaration of the Rights of Man and Citizen is considered by many to be the key philosophical document of the French Revolution. The declaration was adopted by the French National Assembly on August 26, 1789, and represented a rejection of the rule of absolute monarchy in favor of natural human rights, including fair taxation, self-determination in government, and individual liberty under the rule of law. The declaration was later made the preamble to France's 1791 constitution.

The representatives of the French people, organized in National Assembly, considering that ignorance, forgetfulness or contempt of the rights of man, are the sole causes of the public miseries and of the corruption of governments, have resolved to set forth in a solemn declaration the natural, inalienable and sacred rights of man, in order that this declaration, being ever present to all the members of the social body, may unceasingly remind them of their rights and their duties; in order that the acts of the legislative power and those of the executive power may be each moment compared with the aim of every political institution and thereby may be more respected; and in order that the demands of citizens, grounded henceforth upon simple and incontestable principles, may always take the direction of maintaining the constitution and welfare of all.

In consequence, the National Assembly recognizes and declares, in the presence and under the auspices of the Supreme Being, the following rights of man and citizen.

1. Men are born and remain free and equal in rights. Social distinctions can be based only upon public utility.

2. The aim of every political association is the preservation of the natural and imprescriptible [unwritten] rights of man. These rights are liberty, property, security, and resistance to oppression.

3. The source of all sovereignty is essentially in the nation, no body, no individual can exercise authority that does not proceed from it in plain terms.

4. Liberty consists in the power to do anything that does not injure others; accordingly, the exercise of the natural rights of each man has no limits except those that secure to the other members of society the enjoyment of these same rights. These limits can be determined only by law.

5. The law has the right to forbid only such actions as are injurious to society. Nothing can be forbidden that is not interdicted [prohibited] by the law, and no one can be constrained to do that which it does not order.

6. Law is the expression of the general will. All citizens have the right to take part personally, or by their representatives, in its formation. It must be the same for all, whether it protects or punishes. All citizens being equal in its eyes, are equally eligible to all public dignities, places, and employments, according to their capacities, and without other distinction than that of their virtues and their talents.

7. No man can be accused, arrested, or detained, except in the cases determined by the law and according to the forms that it has prescribed. Those who procure [obtain], expedite [hasten], execute, or cause to be executed arbitrary orders ought to be punished: but every citizen summoned or seized in virtue of the law ought to render instant obedience; he makes himself guilty by resistance.

8. The law ought to establish only penalties that are strictly and obviously necessary, and no one can be punished except in virtue of a law established and promulgated [announced] prior to the offence and legally applied.

9. Every man being presumed innocent until he has been pronounced guilty, if it is thought indispensable to arrest him, all severity that may not be necessary to secure his person ought to be strictly suppressed by law.

10. No one should be disturbed on account of his opinions, even religious, provided their manifestation [display] does not derange [disturb] the public order established by law.

11. The free communication of ideas and opinions is one of the most precious of the rights of man; every citizen then can freely speak, write, and print, subject to responsibility for the abuse of this freedom in the cases determined by law.

12. The guarantee of the rights of man and citizen requires a public force; this force then is instituted for the advantage of all and not for the personal benefit of those to whom it is entrusted.

13. For the maintenance of the public force and for the expenses of administration a general tax is indispensable; it ought to be equally apportioned [divided] among all the citizens according to their means.

14. All the citizens have the right to ascertain [determine], by themselves or by their representatives, the necessity of the public tax, to consent to it freely, to follow the employment of it, and to determine the quota, the assessment, the collection, and the duration of it.

15. Society has the right to call for an account of his administration from every public agent.

16. Any society in which the guarantee of the rights is not secured, or the separation of powers not determined, has no constitution at all.

17. Property being a sacred and inviolable [untouchable] right, no one can be deprived of it, unless a legally established public necessity evidently demands it, under the condition of a just and prior indemnity [payment].

≈≈≈≈≈≈≈≈≈≈≈≈≈≈≈≈≈≈≈≈≈≈≈≈≈≈≈≈≈≈≈≈≈≈≈≈≈≈

## THINKING CRITICALLY

1. What are the stated purposes of this document?
2. What does the declaration state in regard to taxation?
3. According to the declaration, what is the purpose of government? How was this idea reflected in the American Declaration of Independence?

# "The Star-Spangled Banner"

During the War of 1812, Francis Scott Key, a Baltimore lawyer, was captured and held aboard a British ship for several days prior to a planned British attack on Baltimore. Key watched the bombardment of the U.S. Fort McHenry from the British ship, but the smoke was so thick that he could not tell who was winning the battle. When at dawn he saw the American flag still flying above the fort, he knew that U.S. forces had held their ground. From the ship, Key wrote the following poem, which was later set to music and became one of the nation's most popular patriotic songs. In 1931 Congress made "The Star-Spangled Banner" the official national anthem of the United States.

Oh, say, can you see, by the dawn's early light,
What so proudly we hailed at the twilight's last
gleaming,
Whose broad stripes and bright stars through the
perilous fight,
O'er the ramparts we watched were so gallantly
streaming?
And the rockets' red glare, the bombs bursting in
air,
Gave proof thro' the night that our flag was still
there.
Oh, say, does that star-spangled banner yet wave
O'er the land of the free, and the home of the
brave!

On the shore, dimly seen thro' the mists of the
deep,
Where the foe's haughty host in dread silence
reposes,
What is that which the breeze o'er the towering
steep,
As it fitfully blows, half conceals, half discloses?
Now it catches the gleam of the morning's first
beam,
In full glory reflected, now shines on the stream.
'Tis the star-spangled banner: oh, long may it wave
O'er the land of the free, and the home of the
brave!

And where is that band who so vauntingly swore
That the havoc of war and the battle's confusion
A home and a country should leave us no more?
Their blood has washed out their foul footsteps'
pollution.
No refuge could save the hireling and slave
From the terror of flight, or the gloom of the grave:
And the star-spangled banner in triumph doth wave
O'er the land of the free, and the home of the
brave!

Oh, thus be it ever when freemen shall stand
Between their loved homes and the war's
desolation;
Blest with victory and peace, may the heaven-
rescued land
Praise the power that hath made and preserved us a
nation!
Then conquer we must, when our cause it is just,
And this be our motto: "In God is our trust!"
And the star-spangled banner in triumph doth
wave,
O'er the land of the free, and the home of the
brave!

## THINKING CRITICALLY

1. What do you think is the significance of the flag for Key? Explain what Key means by "the land of the free."

2. To whom is Key referring in the first four lines of the third verse?

3. Some people today believe that "The Star-Spangled Banner" is too difficult a song to sing and that another song should replace it as the U.S. national anthem. Do you agree or disagree? Explain.

# Monroe Doctrine

The Monroe Doctrine, originally delivered as part of President James Monroe's annual address to Congress in 1823, came in response to growing fear that the Holy Alliance of Russia, Prussia, and Austria would aid Spain in a reconquest of the newly established independent republics in Latin America. The Doctrine stated in unmistakable terms that the Western Hemisphere was henceforth completely off-limits to any further European expansion.

A precise knowledge of our relations with foreign powers as respects our negotiations and transactions with each is thought to be particularly necessary. . . .

[T]he occasion has been judged proper for asserting . . . that the American continents, by the free and independent condition which they have assumed and maintain, are henceforth not to be considered as subjects for future colonization by any European powers. . . .

In the wars of the European powers in matters relating to themselves we have never taken any part, nor does it comport [comply] with our policy so to do. It is only when our rights are invaded or seriously menaced that we resent injuries or make preparation for our defense.

With the movements in this hemisphere we are of necessity more immediately connected. . . . We owe it . . . to candor [honest speaking] and to the amicable relations existing between the United States and those [allied] powers to declare that we should consider any attempt on their part to extend their system to any portion of this hemisphere as dangerous to our peace and safety.

With the existing colonies or dependencies of any European power we have not interfered and shall not interfere. But with the governments who have declared their independence and maintained it . . . we could not view any interposition [intrusion] . . . by any European power in any other light than as the manifestation [indication] of an unfriendly disposition toward the United States. . . .

Our policy in regard to Europe, which was adopted at an early stage of the wars . . . remains the same, which is not to interfere in the internal concerns of any of its powers. . . . But . . . it is impossible that the allied powers should extend their political system to any portion of either continent without endangering our peace and happiness; nor can anyone believe that our southern brethren, if left to themselves, would adopt it of their own accord.

It is equally impossible, therefore, that we should behold such interposition in any form with indifference. . . . It is still the true policy of the United States to leave the parties to themselves, in the hope that other powers will pursue the same course.

≈≈≈≈≈≈≈≈≈≈≈≈≈≈≈≈≈≈≈≈≈≈≈≈≈≈≈≈≈≈≈≈≈≈≈≈≈≈≈≈

## THINKING CRITICALLY

1. According to Monroe, in what situations would the United States make preparations for defense?
2. How will the United States view any intrusion upon the safety of an independent nation?
3. To what foreign-policy agenda is Monroe adhering? Explain.

# Seneca Falls Declaration of Women's Rights

In 1848 abolitionists Elizabeth Cady Stanton and Lucretia Mott organized and promoted the first Women's Rights Convention in Seneca Falls, New York. The Declaration of Sentiments and Resolutions adopted at the conference is one of the first documents to demand equal rights for women.

## Declaration of Sentiments

When, in the course of human events, it becomes necessary for one portion of the family of man to assume among the people of the earth a position different from that which they have hitherto occupied . . . a decent respect to the opinions of mankind requires that they should declare the causes that impel them to such a course.

We hold these truths to be self-evident: that all men and women are created equal; that they are endowed by their Creator with certain inalienable rights; that among these are life, liberty, and the pursuit of happiness; that to secure these rights governments are instituted, deriving their just powers from the consent of the governed. . . .

But when a long train of abuses and usurpations [unrightful takings], pursuing invariably the same object, evinces a design [plans] to reduce them under absolute despotism [without freedom], it is their duty to throw off such government and to provide new guards for their future security. Such has been the patient sufferance of the women under this government, and such is now the necessity which constrains them to demand the equal station to which they are entitled.

The history of mankind is a history of repeated injuries and usurpations on the part of man toward woman, having in direct object the establishment of an absolute tyranny over her. To prove this, let facts be submitted to a candid world.

He has never permitted her to exercise her inalienable right to the elective franchise [vote].

He has compelled her to submit to laws, in the formation of which she had no voice.

He has withheld from her rights which are given to the most ignorant and degraded men. . . .

Having deprived her of this first right of a citizen . . . he has oppressed her on all sides.

He has made her, if married, in the eye of the law, civilly dead.

He has taken from her all right in property, even to the wages she earns.

In the covenant of marriage, she is compelled to promise obedience to her husband, he becoming, to all intents and purposes, her master—the law giving him power to deprive her of her liberty, and to administer chastisement. . . .

[I]f [she is] single and the owner of property, he has taxed her to support a government which recognizes her only when her property can be made profitable to it.

He has monopolized nearly all the profitable employments. . . .

He has denied her the facilities for obtaining a thorough education, . . .

He has endeavored, in every way that he could, to destroy her confidence in her own powers, to lessen her self-respect, and to make her willing to lead a dependent and abject [spiritless] life.

Now, in view of this entire disfranchisement of one-half the people of this country . . . we insist that they have immediate admission to all the rights and privileges which belong to them as citizens of the United States. . . .

## Resolutions

*Resolved*, that all laws which prevent woman from occupying such a station in society as her conscience shall dictate, or which place her in a position inferior to that of man, are contrary to the great precept of nature and therefore of no force or authority.

*Resolved*, that woman is man's equal. . . .

*Resolved*, that the same amount of virtue, delicacy, and refinement of behavior that is required of woman in the social state should also be required of man. . . .

*Resolved*, that it is the duty of the women in this country to secure to themselves their sacred right to the elective franchise. . . .

*Resolved*, therefore, that, being invested by the Creator with the same capabilities and the same consciousness of responsibility for their exercise, it is demonstrably the right and duty of woman, equally with man, to promote every righteous cause by every righteous means.

## THINKING CRITICALLY

1. Explain the basic objections that the drafters of this declaration have toward the government.

2. According to the declaration, what needs to be done to remedy the unequal situation?

3. Why do you think the drafters of this declaration used language similar to that of the U.S. Declaration of Independence?

# Emancipation Proclamation

The Emancipation Proclamation is often remembered as the declaration that ended slavery. The proclamation did not, however, free a single slave because the areas to which the proclamation applied were under Confederate control. The true effectiveness of the Emancipation Proclamation was its success in boosting Union morale, increasing dissatisfaction in the South, and gaining European support for the Union effort.

Whereas, on the 22nd day of September, in the year of our Lord 1862, a proclamation was issued by the President of the United States, containing, among other things, the following, to wit:

That on the 1st day of January, in the year of our Lord 1863, all persons held as slaves within any state or designated part of a state, the people whereof shall then be in rebellion against the United States, shall be then, thenceforward, and forever free; and the executive government of the United States, including the military and naval authority thereof, will recognize and maintain the freedom of such persons and will do no act or acts to repress such persons, or any of them, in any efforts they may make for their actual freedom.

That the executive will, on the 1st day of January aforesaid, by proclamation, designate the states and parts of states, if any, in which the people thereof respectively, shall then be in rebellion against the United States; and the fact that any state or the people thereof shall on that day be in good faith represented in the Congress of the United States by members chosen thereto at elections wherein a majority of the qualified voters of such states shall have participated shall, in the absence of strong countervailing [contradictory] testimony be deemed conclusive evidence that such state and the people thereof are not then in rebellion against the United States.

Now, therefore, I, Abraham Lincoln, President of the United States, by virtue of the power in me vested as commander in chief of the Army and Navy of the United States, in time of actual armed rebellion against the authority and government of the United States, and as a fit and necessary war measure for suppressing said rebellion, do, on this 1st day of January, in the year of our Lord 1863, and in accordance with my purpose so to do, publicly proclaimed for the full period of 100 days from the day first above mentioned, order and designate as the states and parts of states wherein the people thereof, respectively, are this day in rebellion against the United States the following, to wit:

Arkansas, Texas, Louisiana, . . . Mississippi, Alabama, Florida, Georgia, South Carolina, North Carolina, and Virginia, . . . and which excepted parts are for the present left precisely as if this proclamation were not issued.

And, by virtue of the power and for the purpose aforesaid, I do order and declare that all persons held as slaves within said designated states and parts of states are, and henceforward shall be, free; and that the executive government of the United States, including the military and naval authorities thereof, will recognize and maintain the freedom of said persons.

And I hereby enjoin upon the people so declared to be free to abstain from all violence, unless in necessary self-defense; and I recommend to them that, in all cases when allowed, they labor faithfully for reasonable wages.

And I further declare and make known that such persons of suitable condition will be received into the armed service of the United States. . . .

And upon this act, sincerely believed to be an act of justice, warranted by the Constitution upon military necessity, I invoke the considerate judgment of mankind and the gracious favor of Almighty God.

## THINKING CRITICALLY

1. To whom did the Emancipation Proclamation apply?

2. What opportunity did Lincoln extend for states to prove that they were not in rebellion?

3. What impact do you think the Emancipation Proclamation had on the Civil War?

# Open-Door Policy in China

The Sino-Japanese War of 1894–1895 left China in political and economic turmoil, thus forcing its government to make economic concessions with foreign nations. Despite the fact that the United States had pursued a relatively small amount of trade with China, U.S. officials were disturbed by the possibility that foreign nations might levy discriminatory tariffs and establish trade barriers against the United States. The Open-Door policy, outlined by U.S. Secretary of State John Hay in 1899, was the means used by the United States to secure equal commercial opportunity in the global market.

Earnestly desirous to remove any cause of irritation and to insure at the same time to the commerce of all nations in China . . . that they shall enjoy perfect equality of treatment for their commerce and navigation . . . the government of the United States would be pleased to see His German Majesty's Government give formal assurances and lend its co-operation in securing like assurances from the other interested powers, that each within its respective sphere of whatever influence:

*First.* Will in no way interfere with any treaty port . . . it may have in China.

*Second.* That the Chinese treaty tariff of the time being shall apply to all merchandise landed or shipped to all such ports . . . no matter to what nationality it may belong, and that duties so leviable shall be collected by the Chinese government.

*Third.* That it will levy no higher harbor dues on vessels of another nationality frequenting any port in such "sphere" than shall be levied on vessels of its own nationality. . . .

The recent ukase [official decree] of His Majesty the Emperor of Russia declaring the port of Talien-wan open . . . to the merchant ships of all nations . . . seem[s] to insure the support of the Emperor to the proposed measure. . . .

The commercial interests of Great Britain and Japan will be so clearly served by the desired declaration of intentions, and the views of the governments of these countries as to the desirability of the adoption of measures ensuring the benefits of equality of treatment of all foreign trade throughout China are so similar to those entertained by the United States, that their acceptance of the propositions herein outlined and their co-operation in advocating [supporting] their adoption by the other powers can be confidently expected.

## THINKING CRITICALLY

1. What is the United States asking Germany to do?

2. Why was Hay confident that Great Britain and Japan would agree to the terms of the policy?

3. Given the current economic status of China, do you think it was wise to establish a reciprocal open-door policy? Explain.

# NAACP: The Task for the Future

The National Association for the Advancement of Colored People (NAACP) was established in 1910 for the purpose of achieving equal protection for African Americans under the U.S. Constitution. The following document, drafted in 1919, describes the program by which the NAACP planned to achieve this goal.

First and Foremost among the objectives for 1919 must be the strengthening of the Association's organization and resources. . . . Its chief aims have many times been stated:

1. A vote for every Negro man and woman on the same terms as for white men and women.
2. An equal chance to acquire the kind of an education that will enable the Negro everywhere wisely to use this vote.
3. A fair trial in courts for all crimes of which he is accused, by judges in whose election he has participated. . . .
4. A chance to sit upon the jury which passes judgment upon him.
5. Defense against lynching and burning at the hands of mobs.
6. Equal service on railroad and other public carriers . . . at the same cost and upon the same terms as other passengers.
7. Equal right to the use of public parks, libraries and other community services for which he is taxed.
8. An equal chance for a livelihood in public and private employment.
9. The abolition of color-hyphenation and the substitution of "straight Americanism."

If it were not a painful fact that more than four-fifths of the colored people of the country are denied the above named elementary rights, it would seem an absurdity that an organization is necessary to demand for American citizens the exercise of such rights. . . .

The fight is the Negro's fight. . . . But, it is no less the white man's fight. The common citizenship rights of no group of people, to say nothing of nearly 12,000,000 of them, can be denied with impunity [exception from punishment] to the State and the social order which denies them. . . . Whoso loves America and cherishes her institutions, owes it to himself and his country to join hands with the members of the National Association for the Advancement of Colored People to "Americanize" America and make the kind of democracy we Americans believe in to be the kind of democracy we should have in *fact*, as well as in theory. . . .

Nor should any one be led astray by the tiresome talk about "social equality." Social equality is a private question which may well be left to individual decision. But, the prejudices of individuals cannot be accepted as the controlling policy of a state. The [NAACP] is concerned primarily with *public equality*. . . . The privileges no less than the duties of citizenship belong of right to no *separate class* of the people, but to all people, and to them as *individuals*.

## THINKING CRITICALLY

1. Briefly summarize the goals of the NAACP.
2. Why is the "Negro's fight" also the white person's fight?
3. Explain the difference between social and public equality. Do you think that social equality will naturally evolve when public equality is accepted?

# Truman Doctrine

On March 12, 1947, President Harry S. Truman addressed a joint session of the U.S. Congress to announce that the United States would help defend Greece and Turkey against Communist advances. In what became known as the Truman Doctrine, the president ended the long-term commitment of the United States to isolationism and launched what was to become the U.S. foreign-policy agenda for the next 40 years—containment.

The gravity of the situation which confronts the world today necessitates my appearance before a joint session of the Congress. The foreign policy and the national security of this country are involved. . . .

One of the primary objectives of the foreign policy of the United States is the creation of conditions in which we and other nations will be able to work out a way of life free from coercion. This was a fundamental issue in the war with Germany and Japan. Our victory was won over countries which sought to impose their will and their way of life upon other nations. . . .

At the present moment in world history nearly every nation must choose between alternative ways of life. The choice is too often not a free one.

One way of life is based upon the will of the majority, and is distinguished by free institutions, representative government, free elections, guarantees of individual liberty, freedom of speech and religion, and freedom from political oppression. The second way of life is based upon the will of a minority forcibly imposed upon the majority. It relies upon terror and oppression, a controlled press and radio, fixed elections, and the suppression of personal freedoms.

I believe that it must be the policy of the United States to support free peoples who are resisting attempted subjugation [control] by armed minorities or by outside pressures. I believe that we must assist free peoples to work out their own destinies in their own way. I believe that our help should be primarily through economic and financial aid, which is essential to economic stability and orderly political processes. . . .

It is necessary only to glance at a map to realize that the survival and integrity of the Greek nation are of grave importance in a much wider situation. If Greece should fall under the control of an armed minority, the effect upon its neighbor, Turkey, would be immediate and serious. Confusion and disorder might well spread throughout the entire Middle East. Moreover, the disappearance of Greece as an independent state would have a profound effect upon those countries in Europe whose peoples are struggling against great difficulties to maintain their freedoms and their independence while they repair the damages of war. . . .

Collapse of free institutions and loss of independence would be disastrous not only for them but for the world. . . .

Should we fail to aid Greece and Turkey in this fateful hour, the effect will be far reaching to the West as well as to the East. We must take immediate and resolute [determined] action.

I therefore ask the Congress to provide authority for assistance to Greece and Turkey in the amount of $400 million for the period ending June 30, 1948. . . .

In addition to funds, I ask the Congress to authorize the detail of American civilian and military personnel to Greece and Turkey, at the request of those countries, to assist in the tasks of reconstruction, and for the purpose of supervising the use of such financial and material assistance. . . .

Finally, I ask that the Congress provide authority which will permit the speediest and most effective use . . . . of such funds as may be authorized. . . .

The seeds of totalitarian regimes are nurtured by misery and want. They spread and grow in the evil soil of poverty and strife. They reach their full growth when the hope of a people for a better life has died. We must keep that hope alive.

The free peoples of the world look to us for support in maintaining their freedoms. If we falter in our leadership, we may endanger the peace of the world—and we shall surely endanger the welfare of our own nation.

Great responsibilities have been placed upon us by the swift movement of events. I am confident that the Congress will face these responsibilities squarely.

## THINKING CRITICALLY

1. According to Truman, what is one of the primary objectives of U.S. foreign policy?

2. How does Truman propose to assist people in their struggle for free government? Why?

3. Explain why the Truman Doctrine marked a fundamental change in U.S. foreign policy. Do you think this policy change was wise? Explain.

# Universal Declaration of Human Rights

On December 10, 1948, the General Assembly of the United Nations adopted the Universal Declaration of Human Rights—an assertion of the fundamental rights that should be extended to all citizens of the world. Following the adoption of the declaration, the General Assembly called upon all member nations to display, read, and teach the sentiments expressed in the document.

Whereas recognition of the inherent [inborn] dignity and of the equal and inalienable rights of all members of the human family is the foundation of freedom, justice, and peace in the world, . . . the General Assembly proclaims this Universal Declaration of Human Rights as a common standard of achievement for all peoples and all nations. . . .

### Article 1

All human beings are born free and equal in dignity and rights. They . . . should act towards one another in a spirit of brotherhood.

### Article 2

Everyone is entitled to all the rights and freedoms set forth in this Declaration, without distinction of any kind. . . .

### Article 3

Everyone has the right to life, liberty, and the security of person.

### Article 4

No one shall be held in slavery or servitude; slavery and the slave trade shall be prohibited in all their forms.

### Article 5

No one shall be subjected to torture or to cruel, inhuman, or degrading treatment or punishment.

### Article 6

Everyone has the right to recognition everywhere as a person before the law.

### Article 7

All are equal before the law and are entitled without any discrimination to equal protection of the law. . . .

### Article 11

Everyone charged with a penal [punishable] offense has the right to be presumed innocent until proved guilty according to law in a public trial at which he has had all the guarantees necessary for his defense. . . .

### Article 12

No one shall be subjected to arbitrary interference with his privacy, family, home or correspondence, nor to attacks upon his honor and reputation. . . .

### Article 13

1. Everyone has the right to freedom of movement and residence within the borders of each State.
2. Everyone has the right to leave any country, including his own, and to return to his country. . . .

### Article 15

1. Everyone has the right to [his own] nationality.
2. No one shall be arbitrarily deprived of his nationality nor denied the right to change his nationality.

### Article 16

Men and women of full age, without any limitation due to race, nationality, or religion, have the right to marry and to found a family. . . .

### Article 17

Everyone has the right to own property. . . .

### Article 18

Everyone has the right to freedom of thought, conscience, and religion. . . .

### Article 19

Everyone has the right to freedom of opinion and expression. . . .

### Article 20

1. Everyone has the right to freedom of peaceful assembly and association.
2. No one may be compelled to belong to an association.

### Article 21

1. Everyone has the right to take part in the government of his country, directly or through freely chosen representatives. . . .
3. The will of the people shall be the basis of the authority of the government; this will shall be expressed in periodic and genuine elections which shall be by universal and equal suffrage and shall be held by secret vote or by equivalent free voting procedures. . . .

### Article 23

1. Everyone has the right to work, to free choice of employment, to just and favorable conditions of work, and to protection against unemployment.
2. Everyone, without any discrimination, has the right to equal pay for equal work. . . .

### Article 25

Everyone has the right to a standard of living adequate for the health and well-being of himself and of his family. . . .

### Article 26

Everyone has the right to education. . . . Elementary education shall be compulsory. . . .

### Article 27

Everyone has the right freely to participate in the cultural life of the community. . . .

### Article 29

Everyone has duties to the community in which alone the free and full development of his personality is possible.

---

## THINKING CRITICALLY

1. What is the stated purpose of the Universal Declaration of Human Rights?
2. How does this declaration compare to the U.S. Bill of Rights?
3. What form of government does the Universal Declaration call for? Provide a specific example from the excerpt to support your answer.

# U.S. Presidential Oath of Office

The inauguration of the president of the United States will always be a milestone event for the nation and, in many ways, for the world. The Inauguration Day ceremony, which is held on a large, flag-draped platform set up at the Capitol on January 20th of every fourth year, represents the beginning of one person's four-year commitment to act as chief executive for the nation as a whole.

According to Article II of the U.S. Constitution, the president-elect must make the following affirmation before taking office.

I do solemnly swear (or affirm) that I will faithfully execute the office of President of the United States, and will, to the best of my ability, preserve, protect, and defend the Constitution of the United States.

It is customary, though not officially required, for the phrase "So help me God" to be added to the end of the oath. In the ceremony, the president-elect recites the oath with his or her left hand on the Bible and right hand slightly raised. Following the oath of office, the president then delivers an Inaugural Address, a speech listened to by people throughout the world.

≈≈≈≈≈≈≈≈≈≈≈≈≈≈≈≈≈≈≈≈≈≈≈≈≈≈≈≈≈≈≈≈≈≈≈≈≈

## THINKING CRITICALLY

1. In your own words, explain the promise that the president-elect is making by reciting the oath of office.

2. To whom is the president-elect making this promise?

3. Why do you think the founders of this nation included the presidential oath of office in the U.S. Constitution?

# Documents of Patriotism

The United States is celebrated for its devotion to the freedom of its people, its cultural and social diversity, and its democratic ideals and institutions. Efforts to preserve and improve the nation bind U.S. citizens together in both patriotic spirit and action. Throughout U.S. history various documents have been written to express that patriotism. Three such documents are the Pledge of Allegiance, the American's Creed, and the Oath of Citizenship.

The first written version of the Pledge of Allegiance appeared in the magazine *Youth's Companion* in 1892. The current version, shown here, was adopted by Congress in 1954. In 1917, William Tyler Page, Clerk of the House of Representatives, presented the American's Creed to the House, which adopted it on behalf of the American people on April 13, 1918. Another statement of U.S. allegiance, the Oath of Citizenship, is recited at the swearing-in ceremony of immigrants who have been granted the privilege of U.S. citizenship.

## Pledge of Allegiance

I pledge allegiance to the flag of the United States of America and to the republic for which it stands, one nation under God, indivisible, with liberty and justice for all.

## American's Creed

I believe in the United States of America as a government of the people, by the people, for the people; whose just powers are derived from the consent of the governed; a democracy in a republic; a sovereign Nation of many sovereign States; a perfect union, one and inseparable; established upon those principles of freedom, equality, justice, and humanity for which American patriots sacrificed their lives and fortunes. I therefore believe it is my duty to my country to love it, to support its Constitution, to obey its laws, to respect its flag, and to defend it against all enemies.

## Oath of Citizenship

I hereby declare, on oath, that I absolutely and entirely renounce and abjure [withdraw] all allegiance and fidelity to any foreign prince, potentate, state or sovereignty, to whom or which I have heretofore been a subject or citizen; that I will support and defend the Constitution and laws of the United States of America against all enemies, foreign and domestic; that I will bear true faith and allegiance to the same; that I will bear arms on behalf of the United States when required by the law; that I will perform noncombatant service in the armed forces of the United States when required by the law; that I will perform work of national importance under civilian direction when required by the law; and that I take this obligation freely without any mental reservation or purpose of evasion; so help me God.

## THINKING CRITICALLY

1. What common sentiments do all three of these documents share?
2. What references do all three documents make to the defense of the nation?
3. Do you think that pledges, creeds, and oaths have an impact on an individual's devotion to his or her country? Explain.

# Patrick Henry's Speech Before the Virginia Convention

On March 23, 1775, Patrick Henry, often referred to as the "Orator of Liberty," addressed the Second Virginia Convention. Convinced that war with Great Britain was inevitable, Henry tried to persuade conservative delegates opposed to the organization of a militia as a means of stopping British tyranny that freedom would be achieved only through revolution.

Mr. President: No man thinks more highly than I do of the patriotism, as well as abilities, of the very worthy gentlemen who have just addressed the House. But different men often see the same subjects in different lights; and, therefore, I hope, it will not be thought disrespectful to those gentlemen if, entertaining as I do, opinions of a character very opposite to theirs, I shall speak forth my sentiments freely and without reserve. . . . For my own part I consider it as nothing less than a question of freedom or slavery. . . .

Mr. President, it is natural to man to indulge in the illusions of hope. We are apt to shut our eyes against a painful truth, and listen to the song of that siren till she transforms us into beasts. Is this the part of wise men, engaged in a great and arduous [difficult] struggle for liberty? Are we disposed to be of the number of those who, having eyes, see not, and having ears, hear not the things which so nearly concern their temporal salvation? For my part, whatever anguish of spirit it may cost, I am willing to know the whole truth; to know the worst and to provide for it.

I have but one lamp by which my feet are guided, and that is the lamp of experience. I know of no way of judging of the future but by the past. And judging by the past, I wish to know what there has been in the conduct of the British ministry for the last ten years to justify those hopes with which gentlemen have been pleased to solace [comfort] themselves and the House [convention]? Is it that insidious [treacherous] smile with which our petition has been lately received? Trust it not, sir; it will prove a snare to your feet. Suffer not yourselves to be betrayed with a kiss. Ask yourselves how this gracious reception of our petition comports [agrees] with those warlike preparations which cover our waters and darken our land. Are fleets and armies necessary to a work of love and reconciliation? Have we shown ourselves so unwilling to be reconciled that force must be called in to win back our love? Let us not deceive ourselves, sir. These are the implements of war and subjugation, the last arguments to which kings resort.

I ask, gentlemen, sir, what means this martial array if its purpose be not to force us to submission? . . . They are meant for us; they can be meant for no other. . . . And what have we to oppose to them? Shall we try argument? Sir, we have been trying that for the last ten years. . . . Sir, we have done everything that could be done to avert the storm which is now coming on. . . .

There is no longer any room for hope. If we wish to be free, . . . if we mean not basely to abandon the noble struggle in which we have been so long engaged and which we have pledged ourselves never to abandon until the glorious object of our contest shall be obtained, we must fight! I repeat it, sir—we must fight! . . .

They tell us, sir, that we are weak, unable to cope with so formidable an adversary. But when shall we be stronger? Will it be the next week or the next year? Will it be when we are totally disarmed and when a British guard shall be stationed in every house? . . . Sir, we are not weak, if we make a proper use of those means which the God of nature hath placed in our power. Three millions of people armed in the holy cause of liberty and in such a country as that which we possess are invincible by any force which our enemy can send against us. . . . There is no retreat but in submission and slavery!

Our chains are forged. Their clanking may be heard on the plains of Boston! The war is inevitable—and let it come! I repeat it, sir—let it come! . . .

Gentlemen may cry peace, peace. But there is no peace. The war is actually begun! Our brethren are already in the field! . . . Is life so dear, or peace so sweet, as to be purchased at the price of chains and slavery? Forbid it, Almighty God! I know not what course others may take; but as for me, give me liberty or give me death!

≈≈≈≈≈≈≈≈≈≈≈≈≈≈≈≈≈≈≈≈≈≈≈≈≈≈≈≈≈≈≈≈≈≈≈

## THINKING CRITICALLY

1. How does Henry demonstrate that the British government cannot be trusted?

2. What is Henry asking the people to do?

3. Explain the basis of the emotional appeal that Henry is making. Which lines in the excerpt do you think are the most convincing?

# Debate on the Proposed Constitution

Among the topics of heated debate at the state ratifying conventions held to determine the future of the U.S. Constitution was the degree of power held by the federal and state governments. At the Virginia ratifying convention, held in June of 1788, Antifederalist Patrick Henry and Federalist James Madison debated the issue of "We the States" versus "We the People."

### Patrick Henry

Mr. Chairman—The public mind, as well as my own, is extremely uneasy at the proposed change of Government. . . . I consider myself as the servant of the people of this Commonwealth, as a centinel [guardian] over their rights, liberty, and happiness. I represent their feelings when I say, that they are exceedingly uneasy, being brought from that state of full security, which they enjoyed, to the present delusive appearance of things. . . . I conceive the republic to be in extreme danger. If our situation be thus uneasy, whence has arisen this fearful jeopardy? It arises from this fatal system—it arises from a proposal to change our government. . . . If a wrong step be now made, the republic may be lost forever. If this new Government will not come up to the expectation of the people, and they should be disappointed—their liberty will be lost, and tyranny must and will arise. I repeat it again, and I beg Gentlemen to consider, that a wrong step made now will plunge us into misery, and our Republic will be lost. . . . And here I would make this enquiry of those worthy characters who composed a part of the late Federal Convention. I am sure they were fully impressed with the necessity of forming a great consolidated Government, instead of a confederation. That this is a consolidated Government is demonstrably clear, and the danger of such a Government, is, to my mind, very striking. I have the highest veneration [regard] for those Gentlemen,—but, Sir, give me leave to demand, what right had they to say, *We, the People*. My political curiosity, exclusive of my anxious solicitude [concern] for the public welfare, leads me to ask, who authorised them to speak the language of, *We, the People*, instead of, *We, the States*? States are the characteristics, and the soul of a confederation. If the States be not the agents of this compact, it must be one great consolidated National Government of the people of all the States. I have the highest respect for those Gentlemen who formed the Convention, and were some of them not here, I would express some testimonial of my esteem for them. America had on a former occasion put the utmost confidence in them: A confidence which was well placed: And I am sure, Sir, I would give up any thing to them; I would chearfully confide in them as my Representatives. But, Sir, on this great occasion, I would demand [to know] the cause of their conduct. . . . The people gave them no power to use their name. That they exceeded their power is perfectly clear. It is not mere curiosity that actuates [motivates] me. I wish to hear the real actual existing danger, which should lead us to take those steps so dangerous in my conception. Disorders have arisen in other parts of America, but here, Sir, no insurrection or tumult, has happened—every thing has been calm and tranquil. But notwithstanding this, we are wandering on the great ocean of human affairs. I see no landmark to guide us. We are running we know not whither. Difference in opinion has gone to a degree of inflammatory resentment in different parts of the country—which has been occasioned [caused] by this perilous innovation. The Federal Convention ought to have amended the old system—for this purpose they were solely delegated. The object of their mission extended to no other consideration. You must therefore forgive the solicitation [request] of one unworthy member, to know what danger could have arisen under the present confederation, and what are the causes of this proposal to change our Government.

**James Madison**

I must take the liberty to make some observations on what was said by another Gentleman, (Mr. Henry). He told us, that this Constitution ought to be rejected, because it endangered the public liberty, in his opinion, in many instances. Give me leave to make one answer to that observation—Let the dangers which this system is supposed to be replete with [full of], be clearly pointed out. If any dangerous and unnecessary powers be given to the general Legislature, let them be plainly demonstrated, and let us not rest satisfied with general assertions of dangers, without examination. . . . He informs us that the people of this country are at perfect repose [peace];—that every man enjoys the fruits of his labor, peaceably and securely, and that every thing is in perfect tranquillity and safety. I wish sincerely, Sir, this were true. If this be their happy situation, why has every State acknowledged the contrary? Why were deputies from all the States sent to the General Convention? . . . Give me leave to say something of the nature of the Government. . . . There are a number of opinions; but the principle question is, whether it be a federal or consolidated Government: In order to judge properly of the question before us, we must consider it minutely in its principle parts. I conceive myself, that it is of a mixed nature:—It is in a manner unprecedented: We cannot find one express example in the experience of the world:—It stands by itself. In some respects, it is a Government of a federal nature; in others it is of a consolidated nature. . . . Who are parties to it? The people—but not the people as composing one great body—but the people as composing thirteen sovereignties: Were it as the Gentleman asserts, a consolidated Government, the assent of a majority of the people would be sufficient for its establishment, and as a majority have adopted it already, the remaining States would be bound by the act of the majority, even if they unanimously reprobated it [considered it unacceptable]: Were it such a Government as it is suggested, it would be now binding on the people of this State, without having had the privilege of deliberating upon it: But, Sir, no State is bound by it, as it is, without its own consent. Should all the States adopt it, it will then be a Government established by the thirteen States of America, not through the intervention of the Legislatures, but by the people at large.

≈≈≈≈≈≈≈≈≈≈≈≈≈≈≈≈≈≈≈≈≈≈≈≈≈≈≈≈≈≈≈≈≈

## THINKING CRITICALLY

1. What type of government does Henry believe the new Constitution will create?
2. Does Madison argue that the Constitution will create a federal or a consolidated government?
3. Do you think that people in the United States today consider the United States to have a consolidated government or a government of 50 interconnected sovereignties? Explain.

# George Washington's Farewell Address

On September 17, 1796, President George Washington made his final address to the people of the United States. His farewell was in effect a warning to the American people—a warning against the growth of political parties and, most notably, against the formation of foreign alliances.

A solicitude [anxiety] for your welfare which cannot end but with my life, and the apprehension of danger natural to that solicitude, urge me on an occasion like the present to offer to your solemn contemplation and to recommend to your frequent review some sentiments which are the result of much reflection. . . .

The name of American, which belongs to you in your national capacity, must always exalt [foster] the just pride of patriotism more than any appellation [name] derived from local discriminations. With slight shades of difference, you have the same religion, manners, habits, and political principles. You have in a common cause fought and triumphed together. The independence and liberty you possess are the work of joint councils and joint efforts, of common dangers, sufferings, and successes. . . .

In this sense it is that your union ought to be considered as a main prop of your liberty, and that the love of the one ought to endear to you the preservation of the other. . . .

In contemplating the causes which may disturb our union, it occurs as matter of serious concern that any ground should have been furnished for characterizing parties by *geographical* discriminations—*Northern* and *Southern, Atlantic* and *Western*—whence designing men may endeavor to excite a belief that there is a real difference of local interests and views. One of the expedients [methods] of party to acquire influence within particular districts is to misrepresent the opinions and aims of other districts. You cannot shield yourselves too much against the jealousies and heartburnings which spring from these misrepresentations; they tend to render alien to each other those who ought to be bound together by fraternal affection. . . .

Let me now take a more comprehensive view, and warn you in the most solemn manner against the baneful [destructive] effects of the spirit of party generally.

This spirit, unfortunately, is inseparable from our nature, having its root in the strongest passions of the human mind. It exists under different shapes in all governments, more or less stifled, controlled, or repressed; but in those of the popular form it is seen in its greatest rankness [most extreme form] and is truly their worst enemy. . . .

It serves always to distract the public councils and enfeeble the public administration. It agitates the community with ill-founded jealousies and false alarms; kindles the animosity of one part against another; foments [excites] occasional riot and insurrection. It opens the door to foreign influence and corruption, which find a facilitated access to the government itself through the channels of party passion. Thus the policy and the will of one country are subjected to the policy and will of another. . . .

Against the insidious wiles [sly tricks] of foreign influence (I conjure [beg] you to believe me, fellow citizens) the jealousy [suspicion] of a free people ought to be constantly awake, since history and experience prove that foreign influence is one of the most baneful foes of republican government. But that jealousy, to be useful, must be impartial, else it becomes the instrument of the very influence to be avoided, instead of a defense against it. Excessive partiality for one foreign nation and excessive dislike for another cause those whom they actuate [drive] to see danger only on one side, and serve to veil and even second the arts of influence on the other. Real patriots who may resist the intrigues of the favorite are liable to become suspected and odious [offensive], while its tools and dupes usurp the applause and confidence of the people to surrender their interests.

The great rule of conduct for us in regard to foreign nations is in extending our commercial relations to have with them as little political connection as possible. So far as we have already formed engagements let them be fulfilled with perfect good faith. . . .

It is our true policy to steer clear of permanent alliances with any portion of the foreign world, so far, I mean, as we are now at liberty to do it; for let me not be understood as capable of patronizing infidelity to existing engagements. I hold the maxim no less applicable to public than to private affairs that honesty is always the best policy. I repeat, therefore, let those engagements be observed in their genuine sense. But in my opinion it is unnecessary and would be unwise to extend them.

Harmony, liberal intercourse [dealings] with all nations are recommended by policy, humanity, and interest. But even our commercial policy should hold an equal and impartial hand, neither seeking nor granting exclusive favors or preferences, . . . constantly keeping in view that it is folly in one nation to look for disinterested favors from another; that it must pay with a portion of its independence for whatever it may accept under that character; that by such acceptance it may place itself in the condition of having given equivalents for nominal favors, and yet of being reproached with ingratitude for not giving more. . . .

Though in reviewing the incidents of my administration I am unconscious of intentional error, I am nevertheless too sensible [aware] of my defects not to think it probable that I may have committed many errors. Whatever they may be, I fervently beseech [beg] the Almighty to avert or mitigate [lessen] the evils to which they may tend. I shall also carry with me the hope that my country will never cease to view them with indulgence, and that, after forty-five years of my life dedicated to its service with an upright zeal, the faults of incompetent abilities will be consigned to oblivion, as myself must soon be to the mansions of rest.

## THINKING CRITICALLY

1. According to Washington, why is it dangerous to form attachments to other nations?

2. What does Washington consider the worst enemy of popular forms of government? Why?

3. What type of foreign-policy agenda is Washington advocating? Provide examples from the excerpt to support your answer.

# Thomas Jefferson's First Inaugural Address

In 1801 Thomas Jefferson assumed the office of president of the United States. His election, which occurred in a nation bitterly divided by party politics, marked the first change of political party control of the executive branch. In his inaugural address the Republican president tried to bring a sense of unity to the opposing parties.

Called upon to undertake the duties of the first executive office of our country, I avail myself. . . .

During the contest of opinion through which we have passed, the animation of discussion and of exertions has sometimes worn an aspect which might impose on strangers unused to think freely and to speak and to write what they think; but this being now decided by the voice of the nation . . . all will, of course, arrange themselves under the will of the law, and unite in common efforts for the common good. All, too, will bear in mind this sacred principle, that though the will of the majority is in all cases to prevail, that will to be rightful must be reasonable; that the minority possess their equal rights, which equal law must protect. . . .

Let us, then, fellow citizens, unite with one heart and one mind. Let us restore to social intercourse that harmony and affection without which liberty and even life itself are but dreary things. . . . But every difference of opinion is not a difference of principle.

We have called by different names brethren [brothers] of the same principle. We are all Republicans, we are all Federalists. If there be any among us who would wish to dissolve this Union or to change its republican form, let them stand undisturbed as monuments of the safety with which error of opinion may be tolerated where reason is left free to combat it. . . .

Let us, then, with courage and confidence pursue our own Federal and Republican principles. . . . [P]ossessing a chosen country, with room enough for our descendants to the hundredth and thousandth generation; entertaining a due sense of our equal right to the use of our own faculties, to the acquisitions of our own industry, to honor and confidence from our fellow citizens, resulting not from birth but from our actions and their sense of them; enlightened by a benign religion, professed, indeed, and practised in various forms, yet all of them inculcating [including] honesty, truth, temperance, gratitude, and the love of man; acknowledging and adoring an overruling Providence which by all its dispensations proves that it delights in the happiness of man here and his greater happiness hereafter; with all these blessings, what more is necessary to make us a happy and prosperous people?

≈≈≈≈≈≈≈≈≈≈≈≈≈≈≈≈≈≈≈≈≈≈≈≈≈≈≈≈≈≈≈≈≈≈≈≈

## THINKING CRITICALLY

1. What does Jefferson say concerning the will of the majority?

2. What is Jefferson asking the people to do?

3. Compare Jefferson's remarks with the current state of party politics in the United States. Do you think that Jefferson's vision of opposing parties working together for the good of the nation is possible? Why or why not?

# Abraham Lincoln's Gettysburg Address

In celebration of the Union victory at the Battle of Gettysburg, a national cemetery was created in Gettysburg, Virginia. On November 19, 1863, the nation's most distinguished leaders gathered for the ceremonial dedication of the National Soldiers' Cemetery. Following a two-hour speech by former Massachusetts senator Edward Everett, considered one of the country's greatest orators, President Abraham Lincoln took the podium. In just three minutes, he had concluded. The next day, Everett wrote Lincoln a note stating that he wished he could flatter himself by thinking he had come as close to "the central idea of the occasion" in two hours as Lincoln had in only a few minutes.

Four score and seven years ago our fathers brought forth on this continent a new nation, conceived in liberty and dedicated to the proposition that all men are created equal.

Now we are engaged in a great civil war, testing whether that nation or any nation so conceived and so dedicated can long endure. We are met on a great battlefield of that war. We have come to dedicate a portion of that field as a final resting place for those who here gave their lives that that nation might live. It is altogether fitting and proper that we should do this.

But, in a larger sense, we cannot dedicate— we cannot consecrate [give to a good purpose]— we cannot hallow—this ground. The brave men, living and dead, who struggled here have conse- crated it far above our poor power to add or detract. The world will little note nor long remember what we say here, but it can never forget what they did here. It is for us, the living, rather, to be dedicated here to the unfinished work which they who fought here have thus far so nobly advanced.

It is rather for us to be here dedicated to the great task remaining before us—that from these honored dead we take increased devotion to that cause for which they gave the last full measure of devotion; that we here highly resolve that these dead shall not have died in vain; that this nation, under God, shall have a new birth of freedom; and that government of the people, by the people, for the people shall not perish from the earth.

## THINKING CRITICALLY

1. Why does Lincoln say that neither he nor the other speakers can consecrate the battlefield?

2. According to Lincoln, what must the people do to honor those who had lost their lives?

3. What do you think Everett meant by "the central idea of the occasion"?

# Susan B. Anthony on Women's Suffrage

Forty years after the Seneca Falls Declaration of Women's Rights, women in the United States still were deprived of the fundamental right of suffrage. In the following statement, made before a Senate committee in 1884, Susan B. Anthony testifies in favor of a constitutional amendment extending the right to vote to U.S. women. It would be more than 30 years after this testimony, however, before women finally achieved suffrage.

The theory of this Government from the beginning has been perfect equality to all the people. . . . But instead of adopting a practice in conformity with the theory of our Government, we began first by saying that all men of property were the people of the nation upon whom the Constitution conferred [gave] equality of rights. The next step was that all white men were the people to whom should be practically applied the fundamental theories. There we halt to-day and stand at a deadlock, so far as the application of our theory may go. We women have been standing before the American republic for thirty years, asking the men to take yet one step further and extend the practical application of the theory of equality of rights to all the people to the other half of the people—the women. That is all that I stand here to-day to attempt to demand. . . .

You deny to me my liberty, my freedom, if you say that I shall have no voice whatever in making, shaping, or controlling the conditions of society in which I live. . . .

The franchise [vote] to you men is not secure. You hold it to-day . . . but if at any time . . .

the majority of any of the States should choose to amend the State constitution so as to disfranchise this or that portion of the white men by making this or that condition, by all the decisions of the Supreme Court and by the legislation thus far there is nothing to hinder them.

Therefore the women demand a sixteenth amendment to bring to women the right to vote . . . and to secure men in their right, because you are not secure. . . .

The amendment which has been presented before you reads:

**Article XVI**

Section 1. The right of suffrage in the United States shall be based on citizenship, and the right of citizens of the United States to vote shall not be denied or abridged by the United States, or by any State, on account of sex, or for any reason not equally applicable to all citizens of the United States.

Section 2. Congress shall have power to enforce this article by appropriate legislation.

≈≈≈≈≈≈≈≈≈≈≈≈≈≈≈≈≈≈≈≈≈≈≈≈≈≈≈≈≈≈≈≈≈≈≈≈≈≈≈≈≈≈

## THINKING CRITICALLY

1. According to Anthony, on what is the U.S. theory of government based?

2. How does Anthony try to convince men that they too will benefit from the proposed amendment?

3. How was the type of government practiced by the United States in theory contradictory to that which it practiced in fact?

# William Jennings Bryan's
# "Cross of Gold"

At the Democratic Convention of 1896 delegates gathered to nominate their candidate for the presidency. The pressing issue of the time, the adoption of the silver standard to replace the expensive gold standard, became the central focus of the convention. William Jennings Bryan, a supporter of the silver standard, delivered the following explanation of the need for currency reform and secured the Democratic nomination for the U.S. presidency.

I come to speak to you in defense of a cause as holy as the cause of liberty—the cause of humanity. . . .

On the fourth of March 1893, a few Democrats, most of them members of Congress, issued an address to the Democrats of the nation, asserting that the money question was the paramount issue of the hour; declaring that a majority of the Democratic party had the right to control the action of the party on this paramount issue; and concluding with the request that the believers in the free coinage of silver in the Democratic party should organize, take charge of, and control the policy of the Democratic party. Three months later, at Memphis, an organization was perfected, and the silver Democrats went forth . . . declaring that, if successful, they would crystallize into a platform the declaration which they had made. Then began the struggle. . . . Our silver Democrats went forth from victory unto victory . . . to enter up the judgment already rendered by the plain people of this country. In this contest, brother has been arrayed against brother, father against son . . . old leaders have been cast aside when they have refused to give expression to the sentiments of those whom they would lead, and new leaders have sprung up to give direction to this cause of truth. Thus has the contest been waged, and we have assembled here under as binding and solemn instructions as were ever imposed upon representatives of the people. . . .

When you [the gold delegates] come before us and tell us that we are about to disturb your business interests, we . . . say to you that you have made the definition of a businessman too limited in its application. The man who is employed for wages is as much a businessman as his employer. . . .

And now, my friends, let me come to the paramount issue. . . . [I]f protection has slain its thousands, the gold standard has slain its tens of thousands. . . .

If the gold standard is a good thing, we ought to declare in favor of its retention and not in favor of abandoning it; and if the gold standard is a bad thing, why should we wait until other nations are willing to help us to let go? . . . If they tell us that the gold standard is the standard of civilization, we reply to them that this, the most enlightened of all the nations of the earth, has never declared for a gold standard and that both the great parties this year are declaring against it. . . . They will search the pages of history in vain to find a single instance where the common people of any land have ever declared themselves in favor of the gold standard. They can find where the holders of fixed investments have declared for a gold standard, but not where the masses have. . . .

The sympathies of the Democratic party, as shown by the platform, are on the side of the struggling masses who have ever been the foundation of the Democratic party. . . .

My friends, we declare that this nation is able to legislate for its own people on every question, without waiting for the aid or consent of any other nation on earth; and upon that issue we expect to carry every State in the Union. It is the issue of 1776 over again. Our ancestors, when but three millions in number, had the courage to declare their political independence of every other nation; shall we, their descendants, when we have grown to seventy millions, declare that we are less independent than our forefathers? No, my friends, that will never be the verdict of our people. Therefore, we care not upon what lines the battle is fought. If they say bimetalism [dual standard of gold and silver] is good, but that we cannot have it until other nations help us, we reply that, instead of having a gold standard because England has, we will restore bimetalism, and then let England have bimetalism because the United States has it. If they dare to come out in the open field and defend the gold standard as a good thing, we will fight them to the uttermost. Having behind us the producing masses of this nation and the world, supported by the commercial interests, the laboring interests, and the toilers everywhere, we will answer their demand for a gold standard by saying to them: You shall not press down upon the brow of labor this crown of thorns, you shall not crucify mankind upon a cross of gold.

## THINKING CRITICALLY

1. According to Bryan, who favored the silver standard and who favored the gold standard?

2. What complaint does Bryan make about the gold delegates' definition of a businessman?

3. Why do you think Bryan addresses the issue of independence?

# Theodore Roosevelt's "New Nationalism"

In 1910 President Theodore Roosevelt, an advocate of business reform, delivered the following speech. Roosevelt's "New Nationalism," as it became known, was an appeal for increased governmental involvement in U.S. business.

We come here today to commemorate one of the epoch-making events . . . [in] the long struggle for the rights of man. . . . Our country—this great republic—means nothing unless it means the triumph of a real democracy, the triumph of popular government, and, in the long run, of an economic system under which each man shall be guaranteed the opportunity to show the best that there is in him. . . .

At many stages in the advance of humanity, [the] conflict between the men who possess more than they have earned and the men who have earned more than they possess is the central condition of progress. . . . [T]he essence of the struggle is to equalize opportunity, destroy privilege, and give to the life and citizenship of every individual the highest possible value. . . .

Now, this means that our government, national and state, must be freed from the sinister influence or control of special interests. . . . [T]he great special business interests too often control and corrupt the men and methods of government for their own profit. . . . Every special interest is entitled to justice . . . but not one is entitled to a vote in Congress. . . . The Constitution guarantees protection to property, and we must make that promise good. But it does not give the right of suffrage to any corporation. . . .

There can be no effective control of corporations while their political activity remains. . . .

We must have complete and effective publicity [openness] of corporate affairs, so that the people may know beyond peradventure [doubt] whether the corporations obey the law and whether their management entitles them to the confidence of the public. It is necessary that laws should be passed to prohibit the use of corporate funds directly or indirectly for political purposes; it is still more necessary that such laws should be thoroughly enforced. . . .

We grudge no man a fortune which represents his own power and sagacity [wisdom], when exercised with entire regard to the welfare of his fellows. We grudge no man a fortune in civil life if it is honorably obtained and well used. We should permit it to be gained only so long as the gaining represents benefit to the community. This, I know, implies a policy of far more active governmental interference with social and economic conditions in this country than we have yet had, but I think we have got to face the fact that such an increase in governmental control is now necessary. . . .

The American people are right in demanding that New Nationalism, without which we cannot hope to deal with new problems.

---

## THINKING CRITICALLY

1. What is Roosevelt's main complaint against corporations?
2. For what is Roosevelt calling?
3. How does Roosevelt give the responsibility of checking unfair business practices back to the people? Do you think this will be effective?

# Woodrow Wilson's "New Freedom"

President Woodrow Wilson, like Thomas Jefferson and Andrew Jackson before him, was strongly opposed to the undue influence wielded by monopolies and trusts. In the following 1912 campaign speech, Wilson describes the need for equality of opportunity in the U.S. economic system.

Gentlemen say . . . that trusts are inevitable . . . they say that the particular kind of combinations that are now controlling our economic development came into existence naturally and were inevitable; and that, therefore, we have to accept them as unavoidable and administer our development through them. . . .

The development of business upon a great scale, upon a great scale of co-operation, is inevitable, and, let me add, is probably desirable. But that is a very different matter from the development of trusts, because the trusts have not grown. They have been artificially created . . . by . . . the deliberate planning . . . of men who were more powerful than their neighbors in the business world, and who wished to make their power secure against competition. . . .

Did you ever look into the way a trust was made? It is very natural, in one sense, in the same sense in which human greed is natural. If I haven't efficiency enough to beat my rivals, then the thing I am inclined to do is to get together with my rivals and say: "Don't let's cut each other's throats; let's combine and determine prices for ourselves; determine the output, and thereby determine the prices: and dominate and control the market." That is very natural. . . . I admit that any large corporation built up by the legitimate processes of business, by economy, by efficiency, is natural; and I am not afraid of it, no matter how big it grows. It can stay big only by doing its work more thoroughly than anybody else. . . .

A trust is formed in this way: a few gentlemen "promote" it. . . . The argument of the promoters is, . . . we will assign to you as your share in the pool twice, three times, four times, or five times what you could have sold your business for to an individual competitor who would have to run it on an economic and competitive basis. We can afford to buy it at such a figure because we are shutting out competition. We can afford to make the stock of the combination half a dozen times what it naturally would be and pay dividends on it, because there will be nobody to dispute the prices we shall fix. . . .

You know, of course, how the little man is crushed by the trusts. He gets a local market. The big concerns come in and undersell him in his local market, and that is the only market he has; if he cannot make a profit there, he is killed. . . . Unless you have unlimited capital (which of course you wouldn't have when you were beginning) or unlimited credit (which these gentlemen can see to it that you shan't get), they can kill you out in local market any time they try . . . for they can sell at a loss in your market because they are selling at a profit everywhere else, and they can recoup the losses by which they beat you by the profits which they make in fields where they have beaten other fellows and put them out. If ever a competitor who by good luck has plenty of money does break into the wider market, then the trust has to buy him out, paying three or four times what the business is worth. Following such a purchase, it has got to pay the interest on the price it has paid for the business, and it has got to tax the whole people of the United States, in order to pay the interest on what it borrowed to do that, or on the stocks and bonds it issued to do it with. Therefore the big trusts, the big combinations, are the most wasteful, the most uneconomical, and, after they pass a certain size, the most inefficient, way of conducting the industries of this country.

A notable example is the way in which Mr. [Andrew] Carnegie was bought out of the steel business. Mr. Carnegie could build better mills and make better steel rails and make them cheaper than anybody else. . . . They didn't dare leave him outside. He had so much more brains in finding out the best processes; he had so much more shrewdness in surrounding himself with the most successful assistants. . . . And they bought him out at a price that amounted to three or four times—I believe actually five times—the estimated value of his properties and of his business, because they couldn't beat him in competition. And then in what they charged afterward for their product—the product of his mills included—they made us pay the interest on the four or five times the difference.

That is the difference between a big business and a trust. A trust is an arrangement to get rid of competition, and a big business is a business that has survived competition by conquering in the field of intelligence and economy. . . . I am for big business, and I am against trusts. Any man who can survive by his brains, any man who can put the others out of the business by making the thing cheaper to the consumer at the same time that he is increasing its intrinsic [real] value and quality, I take off my hat to, and I say: "You are the man who can build up the United States, and I wish there were more of you." . . .

The only thing that can ever make a free country is to keep a free and hopeful heart under every jacket in it. Honest American industry has always thriven, when it has thriven at all, on freedom; it has never thriven on monopoly. . . . I am not jealous of the size of any business that has grown to that size. I am not jealous of any process of growth, no matter how huge the result, provided the result was indeed obtained by the processes of wholesome development, which are the processes of efficiency, of economy, of intelligence, and of invention.

## THINKING CRITICALLY

1. How does Wilson distinguish between trusts and big business?
2. According to Wilson, how do trusts harm the consumer?
3. Why are monopolies contrary to U.S. ideals of freedom?

# Woodrow Wilson's "Fourteen Points"

In April 1917 a reluctant President Woodrow Wilson declared war on the Central Powers. The United States had officially entered World War I. On January 18, 1918, Wilson addressed Congress to present what he considered the 14 basic elements needed for a lasting world peace. Wilson's speech launched the idea that democratic foreign policy should be guided by morality and humanitarianism.

We entered this war because violations of right had occurred which touched us to the quick and made the life of our own people impossible unless they were corrected and the world secured once for all against their recurrence. What we demand in this war, therefore, is nothing peculiar to ourselves. It is that the world be made fit and safe to live in. . . . All the peoples of the world are in effect partners in this interest, and for our own part we see very clearly that unless justice be done to others, it will not be done to us. The program of the world's peace, therefore, is our program; and that program, the only possible program, as we see it, is this:

### I.

Open covenants [solemn agreements] of peace. . . .

### II.

Absolute freedom of navigation upon the seas, outside territorial waters. . . .

### III.

The removal, so far as possible, of all economic barriers . . . among all the nations consenting to the peace. . . .

### IV.

Adequate guarantees given and taken that national armaments will be reduced to the lowest point consistent with domestic safety.

### V.

A free, open-minded, and absolutely impartial adjustment of all colonial claims, based upon a strict observance of the principle that in determining all such questions of sovereignty, the interests of the populations concerned must have equal weight with the equitable claims of the government whose title is to be determined.

### VI.

The evacuation of all Russian territory . . . obtaining for her an unhampered and unembarrassed opportunity for the independent determination of her own political development and national policy. . . .

### VII.

Belgium, the whole world will agree, must be evacuated and restored, without any attempt to limit the sovereignty which she enjoys in common with all other free nations. . . .

### VIII.

All French territory should be freed and the invaded portions restored . . . in order that peace may once more be made secure in the interest of all.

### IX.

A readjustment of the frontiers of Italy should be effected along clearly recognizable lines of nationality.

### X.

The peoples of Austria-Hungary . . . should be accorded the freest opportunity of autonomous development.

### XI.

Rumania, Serbia, and Montenegro should be evacuated . . . and international guarantees of the political and economic independence and territorial integrity of the several Balkan states should be entered into.

### XII.

The Turkish portions of the present Ottoman Empire should be assured a secure sovereignty, but the other nationalities which are now under Turkish rule should be assured an undoubted security of life. . . .

### XIII.

An independent Polish state should be erected . . . and . . . political and economic independence and territorial integrity should be guaranteed by international covenant.

### XIV.

A general association of nations must be formed under specific covenants for the purpose of affording mutual guarantees of political independence and territorial integrity to great and small states alike.

In regard to these essential rectifications [corrections] of wrong and assertions of right we feel ourselves to be intimate partners of all the governments and peoples associated together against the Imperialists. . . . We stand together until the end.

For such arrangements and covenants we are willing to fight and to continue to fight until they are achieved; but only because we wish the right to prevail and desire a just and stable peace such as can be secured only by removing the chief provocations to war, which this program does not remove.

We have no jealousy of German greatness, and there is nothing in this program that impairs it. . . . We do not wish to fight her either with arms or with hostile arrangements of trade if she is willing to associate herself with us and the other peace-loving nations of the world in covenants of justice and law and fair dealing. We wish her only to accept a place of equality among the peoples of the world—the new world in which we now live—instead of a place of mastery.

Neither do we presume to suggest to her any alteration or modification of her institutions. But it is necessary . . . that we should know whom her spokesmen speak for when they speak to us. . . .

We have spoken now, surely, in terms too concrete to admit . . . any further doubt or question. An evident principle runs through the whole program I have outlined. It is the principle of justice to all peoples and nationalities, and their right to live on equal terms of liberty and safety with one another, whether they be strong or weak. . . . The people of the United States could act upon no other principle; and to the vindication of this principle they are ready to devote their lives, their honor, and everything that they possess. The moral climax of this, the culminating and final war for human liberty, has come, and they are ready to put their own strength, their own highest purpose, their own integrity and devotion to the test.

## THINKING CRITICALLY

1. What common goal does Wilson address when he discusses the readjustment of all territorial claims?

2. What was Wilson calling for in the fourteenth point of the speech?

3. According to Wilson, why should the United States be concerned about peace in the rest of the world? Do you agree or disagree with this statement? Why?

# Excerpt from a Filibuster

Senate proceedings often have been hampered by the delaying tactic of the filibuster. Although attempts have been made to put an end to the efforts of a minority of senators to block the will of the majority, senators continue to have the right to "talk a bill to death." Some senators have even read from telephone books or almanacs to stall a vote on a bill. The following excerpt from a 1935 session of the Senate, featuring the late Louisiana senator Huey P. Long, is a comical example of a one-man filibuster.

**M**r. Long resumed his speech. After having spoken for about 5 hours, he yielded to Mr. Thomas of Oklahoma, and the following debate ensued:

MR. THOMAS. Mr. President, will the Senator yield?

MR. LONG. I yield.

MR. THOMAS. I suggest the absence of a quorum.

MR. HARRISON. Mr. President, I did not understand the request.

MR. THOMAS. I suggested the absence of a quorum.

MR. HARRISON. Of course, I do not want to interfere with the speech of the Senator from Louisiana, but I will have to insist upon the rules with reference to the speech, that no Senator shall be permitted to speak more than twice in one day on the same subject matter.

MR. LONG. Mr. President, that gives me another speech after this one.

MR. HARRISON. I do not raise the point of order. I am just stating the rule of the Senate in respect to that matter.

MR. LONG. It has never been the rule of the Senate that a quorum call shall be interpreted as bringing a speech to a conclusion. . . .

MR. HARRISON. If the Senator yields for a point of no quorum to be made, does the Chair rule that he can continue his speech under the rule of the Senate that no Senator can speak more than twice on the same subject matter on the same day? . . .

THE VICE PRESIDENT. Under the practice of the Senate a Senator yielding for the purpose of giving another Senator an opportunity of raising the point of no quorum does not yield the floor. That is the universal practice of the Senate. . . .

MR. LONG. Very well. . . . I have spent a number of evenings acquainting people with how to prepare oysters. I had a bucket of oysters sent to me from Louisiana the other night, and I was asked by a very fine bunch of my friends if I would not drop around with the New Orleans oysters and fry some of them for them in good Louisiana style and way. So, Mr. President, I bought a frying pan about 8 inches deep. I bought the frying pan because I was afraid they would not have a frying pan there in which I could fry the oysters. I bought a frying pan, as I said, 8 inches deep and about 17 inches in diameter. . . .

Mr. President, you roll those oysters in the dry meal. You do not want to cook the meal or put water in the meal at any time or anything like that. Just salt the meal and roll the oysters in it. Then, let the grease get boiling hot. You want the grease about 6 inches deep. Then you take the oysters and you place the oysters in the strainer, and you put the strainer in the grease, full depth down to the bottom. Then, you fry those oysters in boiling grease until they turn a gold-copper color and rise to the top, and then, you take them out and let them cool just a little bit before you eat them. . . .

MR. TYDINGS. Mr. President—

THE PRESIDING OFFICER. Does the Senator from Louisiana yield to the Senator from Maryland?

MR. LONG. I yield.

MR. TYDINGS. Does the Senator realize when he describes how these oysters are cooked and how appetizing they seem to be, that those of us who are listening are being inhumanly punished? [Laughter.]

MR. LONG. I had forgotten that. I was trying to make the Senator from Mississippi [Mr. Harrison] hungry. . . .

It is very important that what I say here shall be correctly printed in the Congressional Record and that it shall be taken to heart and learned by every Member of the Senate.

Now, I come to potlikker. Now, I will give my recipe for potlikker. First let me tell Senators what potlikker is. Potlikker is the residue that remains from the commingling, heating, and evaporation [laughter]— anyway, it is in the bottom of the pot! [Laughter.]

Here is how potlikker is made. . . .

When you have cooked the greens until they are tender and the turnips until they are tender, then you take up the turnips and the greens, and the soup that is left is potlikker. [Laughter.]. . . .

Would it be possible to call the roll and ask every Senator who will sit here and listen to me to indicate that he will stay here, and those who will not let them indicate that they will not do so? . . .

THE VICE PRESIDENT. The Chair will say to the Senator that he would have to yield the floor if that were done; but the Chair would suggest to the Senator that he can see the Senators sitting around him and he might ask them individually as to their sentiments.

MR. LONG. Give me the list. I should like to find out if Senators really want to listen to me. The first name on the list is that of the Senator from Colorado [Mr. Adams]. I should like to know if the Senator from Colorado really wants to stay here and listen to me this evening?

MR. LA FOLLETTE. Mr. President, I make the point of order that the Senator from Louisiana cannot yield except for a question.

THE VICE PRESIDENT. The point of order of the Senator from Wisconsin is well taken.

MR. LONG. Very well.

THE VICE PRESIDENT. Any time the Senator from Louisiana yields for anything but a question he loses the floor.

MR. LONG. Very well. I will not yield it, but I was hoping that, by unanimous consent, we could find out about it. I want to find out how popular I am in this body. [Laughter.] I want to know. If it should get back to Louisiana that the Senators are sitting here this evening listening to me, after I had been speaking for 7 hours—. . . .

≈≈≈≈≈≈≈≈≈≈≈≈≈≈≈≈≈≈≈≈≈≈≈≈≈≈≈≈≈≈≈≈≈≈≈≈

## THINKING CRITICALLY

1. According to the debate between Mr. Long and Mr. Harrison, what statutory efforts had Congress made to limit filibusters?

2. Why did Mr. Long want to ask all the members of the Senate what they thought of his speech rather than have a roll call? Why did he want the inquiry in the first place?

3. What possible harms do you see in the practice of filibusters?

# Franklin D. Roosevelt's "Four Freedoms"

In his 1941 annual address to Congress, President Franklin D. Roosevelt discussed the "four freedoms" for which the United States stood. In the midst of the imminent threat of World War II, Roosevelt's speech was an expression of his vision for the social and political future of the United States and the world.

I address you, the members of the Seventy-seventh Congress, at a moment unprecedented in the history of the Union. I use the word "unprecedented," because at no previous time has American security been as seriously threatened from without as it is today. . . .

A free nation has the right to expect full co-operation from all groups. A free nation has the right to look to the leaders of business, of labor, and of agriculture to take the lead in stimulating effort, not among other groups but within their own groups.

The best way of dealing with the few slackers or troublemakers in our midst is, first, to shame them by patriotic example, and if that fails, to use the sovereignty of government to save government.

As men do not live by bread alone, they do not fight by armaments alone. Those who man our defenses, and those behind them who build our defenses, must have the stamina and the courage which come from an unshakable belief in the manner of life which they are defending. The mighty action that we are calling for cannot be based on a disregard of all things worth fighting for.

The Nation takes great satisfaction and much strength from the things which have been done to make its people conscious of their individual stake in the preservation of democratic life in America. Those things have toughened the fiber of our people, have renewed their faith and strengthened their devotion to the institutions we make ready to protect.

Certainly this is no time for any of us to stop thinking about the social and economic problems which are the root cause of the social revolution which is today a supreme factor in the world.

For there is nothing mysterious about the foundations of a healthy and strong democracy. The basic things expected by our people of their political and economic systems are simple. They are: equality of opportunity for youth and for others; jobs for those who can work; security for those who need it; the ending of special privilege for the few; the preservation of civil liberties for all; the enjoyment of the fruits of scientific progress in a wider and constantly rising standard of living.

These are the simple and basic things that must never be lost sight of in the turmoil and unbelievable complexity of our modern world. The inner and abiding strength of our economic and political systems is dependent upon the degree to which they fulfill these expectations. . . .

In the future days, which we seek to make secure, we look forward to a world founded upon four essential human freedoms.

The first is freedom of speech and expression—everywhere in the world.

The second is freedom of every person to worship God in his own way—everywhere in the world.

The third is freedom from want—which, translated into world terms, means economic understandings which will secure to every nation a healthy peacetime life for its inhabitants—everywhere in the world.

The fourth is freedom from fear—which, translated into world terms, means a world-wide reduction of armaments to such a point and in such a thorough fashion that no nation will be in a position to commit an act of physical aggression against any neighbor—anywhere in the world.

That is no vision of a distant millennium. It is a definite basis for a kind of world attainable in our own time and generation. That kind of world is the very antithesis [opposite] of the so-called new order of tyranny which the dictators seek to create with the crash of a bomb.

To that new order we oppose the greater conception—the moral order. A good society is able to face schemes of world domination and foreign revolutions alike without fear.

Since the beginning of our American history, we have been engaged in change—in a perpetual peaceful revolution—a revolution which goes on steadily, quietly adjusting itself to changing conditions—without the concentration camp or the quicklime in the ditch. The world order which we seek is the co-operation of free countries, working together in a friendly, civilized society.

This nation has placed its destiny in the hands and heads and hearts of its millions of free men and women; and its faith in freedom under the guidance of God. Freedom means the supremacy of human rights everywhere. Our support goes to those who struggle to gain those rights or keep them. Our strength is in our unity of purpose.

To that high concept there can be no end save victory.

≈≈≈≈≈≈≈≈≈≈≈≈≈≈≈≈≈≈≈≈≈≈≈≈≈≈≈≈≈≈≈≈≈≈≈≈≈

## THINKING CRITICALLY

1. According to Roosevelt, what do Americans expect from their government?
2. In your own words, describe Roosevelt's four freedoms.
3. For what did Roosevelt claim that the United States was fighting?

# John F. Kennedy's Inaugural Address

On January 20, 1961, John F. Kennedy assumed the office of president of the United States. In his brief yet eloquent inaugural address Kennedy called upon the people of the nation and the world to unite in the pursuit of peace and freedom.

We observe today not a victory of party but a celebration of freedom—symbolizing an end as well as a beginning—signifying renewal as well as change. For I have sworn before you and Almighty God the same solemn oath our forebears prescribed nearly a century and three-quarters ago.

The world is very different now. For man holds in his mortal hands the power to abolish all forms of human poverty and all forms of human life. . . .

We dare not forget today that we are the heirs of that first revolution. Let the word go forth from this time and place, to friend and foe alike, that the torch has been passed to a new generation of Americans . . . unwilling to witness or permit the slow undoing of those human rights to which this nation has always been committed, and to which we are committed today at home and around the world.

Let every nation know, whether it wishes us well or ill, that we shall pay any price, bear any burden, meet any hardship, support any friend, oppose any foe to assure the survival and the success of liberty.

This much we pledge—and more.

To those old allies whose cultural and spiritual origins we share, we pledge the loyalty of faithful friends. United, there is little we cannot do in a host of cooperative ventures. Divided, there is little we can do—for we dare not meet a powerful challenge at odds and split asunder [apart].

To those new states whom we welcome to the ranks of the free, we pledge our word that one form of colonial control shall not have passed away merely to be replaced by a far more iron tyranny. . . .

To those peoples in the huts and villages of half the globe struggling to break the bonds of mass misery, we pledge our best efforts to help them help themselves, for whatever period is required—not because the Communists may be doing it, not because we seek their votes, but because it is right. If a free society cannot help the many who are poor, it cannot save the few who are rich.

To our sister republics south of our border, we offer . . . a new alliance for progress—to assist free men and free governments in casting off the chains of poverty. But this peaceful revolution of hope cannot become the prey of hostile powers. Let all our neighbors know that we shall join with them to oppose aggression or subversion anywhere in the Americas. And let every other power know that this hemisphere intends to remain the master of its own house.

To that world assembly of sovereign states, the United Nations, our last best hope in an age where the instruments of war have far outpaced the instruments of peace, we renew our pledge of support. . . .

Finally, to those nations who would make themselves our adversary [enemy], we offer not a pledge but a request—that both sides begin anew the quest for peace before the dark powers of destruction unleashed by science engulf all humanity in planned or accidental self-destruction. We dare not tempt them with weakness. For only when our arms are sufficient beyond doubt can we be certain beyond doubt that they will never be employed. . . .

So let us begin anew—remembering on both sides that civility is not a sign of weakness, and sincerity is always subject to proof. Let us never negotiate out of fear. But let us never fear to negotiate. . . .

In your hands, my fellow citizens, more than in mine, will rest the final success or failure of our course. Since this country was founded, each generation of Americans has been summoned to give testimony to its national loyalty. The graves of young Americans who answered the call to service surround the globe.

Now the trumpet summons us again . . . to bear the burden of a long twilight struggle, . . . a struggle against the common enemies of man: tyranny, poverty, disease, and war itself. . . .

In the long history of the world, only a few generations have been granted the role of defending freedom in its hour of maximum danger. I do not shrink from this responsibility—I welcome it. I do not believe that any of us would exchange places with any other people or any other generation. The energy, the faith, the devotion which we bring to this endeavor will light our country and all who serve it—and the glow from that fire can truly light the world.

And so, my fellow Americans—ask not what your country can do for you—ask what you can do for your country.

My fellow citizens of the world—ask not what America will do for you but what together we can do for the freedom of man.

Finally, whether you are citizens of America or citizens of the world, ask of us here the same high standards of strength and sacrifice which we ask of you. With a good conscience our only sure reward, with history the final judge of our deeds, let us go forth to lead the land we love, asking His blessing and His help, but knowing that here on earth God's work must truly be our own.

## THINKING CRITICALLY

1. What does Kennedy say regarding the production of armaments? Do you agree or disagree with his point of view?

2. What appeal is Kennedy making to the American people?

3. What is the main focus of Kennedy's speech? Do you think it would be an appropriate inaugural address today? Why or why not?

# Martin Luther King, Jr.'s "I Have a Dream"

On August 28, 1968, on the steps of the Lincoln Memorial in Washington, D.C., more than 200,000 people staged the largest civil rights demonstration in U.S. history. Hoping to encourage the U.S. Congress to finally address the urgent issues of civil rights and equality of opportunity for all, a number of speakers voiced the urgency of reform. In particular, the moving words of Reverend Martin Luther King, Jr., echoed throughout the nation's capital and became a rallying cry for civil rights reform in the United States.

Five score years ago, a great American, in whose symbolic shadow we stand, signed the Emancipation Proclamation. . . . But one hundred years later, we must face the tragic fact that the Negro is still not free. One hundred years later, the life of the Negro is still sadly crippled by the manacles of segregation and the chains of discrimination. One hundred years later, the Negro lives on a lonely island of poverty in the midst of a vast ocean of material prosperity. One hundred years later, the Negro is still languished in the corners of American society and finds himself an exile in his own land. . . .

We have also come to this hallowed spot to remind America of the fierce urgency of now. . . . *Now* is the time to make real the promises of democracy. *Now* is the time to rise from the dark and desolate valley of segregation to the sunlit path of racial justice. *Now* is the time to open the doors of opportunity to all of God's children. . . .

But there is something that I must say to my people. . . . In the process of gaining our rightful place we must not be guilty of wrongful deeds. Let us not seek to satisfy our thirst for freedom by drinking from the cup of bitterness and hatred. We must forever conduct our struggle on the high plane of dignity and discipline. We must not allow our creative protest to degenerate into physical violence. . . .

The marvelous new militancy which has engulfed the Negro community must not lead us to a distrust of all white people, for many of our white brothers, as evidenced by their presence here today, have come to realize that their destiny is tied up with our destiny and their freedom is inextricably bound to our freedom. We cannot walk alone. . . .

There are those who are asking the devotees of civil rights, "When will you be satisfied?"

We can never be satisfied as long as the Negro is the victim of the unspeakable horrors of police brutality.

We can never be satisfied as long as our bodies, heavy with the fatigue of travel, cannot gain lodging in the motels of the highways and the hotels of the cities.

We cannot be satisfied as long as the Negro's basic mobility is from a smaller ghetto to a larger one.

We cannot be satisfied as long as a Negro in Mississippi cannot vote and a Negro in New York believes he has nothing for which to vote. . . .

I say to you today, my friends, that in spite of the difficulties and frustrations of the moment I still have a dream. It is a dream deeply rooted in the American dream.

I have a dream that one day this nation will rise up and live out the true meaning of its creed: "We hold these truths to be self-evident; that all men are created equal." . . .

I have a dream that my four little children will one day live in a nation where they will not be judged by the color of their skin but by the content of their character.

I have a dream today. . . .

I have a dream that . . . the glory of the Lord shall be revealed, and all flesh shall see it together.

This is our hope. This is the faith with which I return to the South. With this faith we will be able to hew out of the mountain of despair a stone of hope. . . .

With this faith we will be able to work together, to pray together, to struggle together, to go to jail together, to stand up for freedom together, knowing that we will be free one day.

This will be the day when all of God's children will be able to sing with new meaning, "My country 'tis of thee, sweet land of liberty, of thee I sing. Land where my fathers died, land of the Pilgrims' pride, from every mountainside, let freedom ring."

And if America is to be a great nation, this must become true. So let freedom ring. . . .

When we let freedom ring, when we let it ring from every village and every hamlet, from every state and every city, we will be able to speed up that day when all of God's children, black men and white men, Jews and Gentiles, Protestants and Catholics, will be able to join hands and sing in the words of the old Negro spiritual, "Free at last! Free at last! Thank God Almighty, we are free at last!"

## THINKING CRITICALLY

1. What does King ask of his fellow African Americans in their struggle for civil rights?
2. Describe King's dream for the nation.
3. What was the significance of the fact that the demonstration was being held at the Lincoln Memorial?

# César Chávez on Nonviolent Protest

As the son of migrant farmworkers and a migrant worker himself, César Chávez had firsthand knowledge of the hardships, poverty, and despair that often characterized the lives of migrant farmworkers in the United States. This knowledge of the conditions under which migrant workers were forced to live and work led Chávez to dedicate his life to improving working conditions for migrant farmworkers. In the early 1960s Chávez's efforts sparked a unionization movement among California farmworkers, leading to the creation of the United Farm Workers union. In the following excerpt from a 1969 open letter to the leaders of the grape industry, against whose products the United Farm Workers had urged a nationwide boycott, Chávez explains the philosophy of nonviolent protest that was at the core of the United Farm Workers union.

Knowing of [Mohandas] Gandhi's admonition [warning] that fasting is the last resort in place of the sword, during a most critical time in our movement last February, I undertook a 25-day fast. I repeat to you the principle enunciated [stated] to the membership at the start of the fast: "If to build our union required the deliberate taking of life, either the life of a grower or his child or the life of a farm worker or his child then I would choose not to see the union built."

We advocate [support] militant nonviolence as our means for social revolution and to achieve justice for our people, but we are not blind or deaf to the desperate and moody winds of human frustration, impatience, and rage that blow among us.

Gandhi himself admitted that if his only choices were cowardice or violence, he would choose violence. Men are not angels and the time and tides wait for no man. Precisely because of these powerful human emotions, we have tried to involve the masses of people in their own struggle. Participation and self-determination remain the best experience of freedom; and free men instinctively prefer democratic change . . . only the enslaved in despair have need of violent overthrow. . . . We hate the agribusiness system that seeks to keep us enslaved, and we shall overcome and change it not by retaliation or bloodshed, but by a determined nonviolent struggle carried on by those masses of farm workers who intend to be free and human.

## THINKING CRITICALLY

1. Why do you think Chávez underwent a 25-day fast?

2. What does Chávez say remains the "best experience of freedom"? Do you agree or disagree with this statement? Explain.

3. Why do you think Chávez included references to Mohandas Gandhi when explaining his philosophy of nonviolent protest? Identify another twentieth-century social reformer who advocated nonviolent protest.

# Spiro T. Agnew's "The Television News Medium"

Vice President Spiro T. Agnew was one of the most outspoken vice presidents in U.S. history. In the following speech, delivered at the Midwest Republican Conference in Des Moines, Agnew launched a verbal attack on the unchecked influence of the television news medium.

Tonight I want to discuss the importance of the television news medium to the American people. . . . No medium has a more profound influence over public opinion. Nowhere in our system are there fewer checks on vast power. So, nowhere should there be more conscientious responsibility exercised than by the news media. The question is, Are we demanding enough of our television news presentations? . . .

The purpose of my remarks tonight is to focus your attention on this little group of men who . . . wield a free hand in selecting, presenting and interpreting the great issues in our nation. . . .

They decide what . . . Americans will learn of the day's events in the nation and in the world.

We cannot measure this power and influence by the traditional democratic standards, for these men can create national issues overnight.

They can make or break by their coverage and commentary a moratorium on the war.

They can elevate men from obscurity to national prominence within a week. They can reward some politicians with national exposure and ignore others. . . .

Now what do Americans know of the men who wield this power? Of the men who produce and direct the network news, the nation knows practically nothing. Of the commentators, most Americans know little other than that they reflect an urbane and assured presence. . . .

The American people would rightly not tolerate this concentration of power in Government.

Is it not fair and relevant to question its concentration in the hands of a tiny, enclosed fraternity of privileged men elected by no one and enjoying a monopoly sanctioned and licensed by Government?

The views of the majority of this fraternity do not—and I repeat, not—represent the views of America. . . .

Now, my friends, we'd never trust such power, as I've described, over public opinion in the hands of an elected Government. It's time we questioned it in the hands of a small and unelected elite.

## THINKING CRITICALLY

1. According to Agnew, what system in U.S. society has the fewest checks on its power?

2. Summarize the problems that Agnew suggests are caused by a powerful television news medium.

3. Do you think that Agnew was correct in his explanation of the vast power of the television news medium? Give examples to support your answer.

# Albert Gore, Jr.'s "Global Environmental Crisis"

The "Earth Summit," held in 1992 in Rio de Janeiro, was an environmental milestone of sorts. Despite its broad agenda, however, little statutory reform actually resulted from the summit. In the following speech to the United Nations in 1993 Vice President Albert Gore, Jr., reminds world leaders of the persistent dangers of the "global environmental crisis."

It is a year since Rio.

And while we usually focus on the ideas expressed during the official proceedings of the Earth Summit, I remember a lot more. . . .

Scientists displayed startlingly beautiful computer images of every square inch of the earth—as seen from space. Artists crafted spectacular sculptures, paintings, music, graphics and films. . . .

All seemed to share a deeper understanding—a recognition that we are all part of something much larger than ourselves, a family related only distantly by blood but intimately by commitment to each other's common future.

And so it is today. We are from different parts of the globe. . . .

But we are united by a common premise: that human activities are needlessly causing grave and perhaps irreparable damage to the global environment.

The dangers are clear to all of us. . . . [F]rom the vast array of problems about which it is possible to be pessimistic, let me mention two.

First, population growth.

It is sobering to realize what is happening to the world's population in the course of our lifetimes.

From the beginnings of the human species until the end of World War II, when I was born, it took more than 10,000 generations to reach a world population of a little more that 2 billion. But in just the past forty-five years, it has gone from a little over 2 billion to 5 1/2 billion.

And if I live another forty-five years, it will be 9 or 10 billion.

The changes brought about by this explosion are not for the distant future. This is not only a problem for our grandchildren.

The problems are already here.

Soil erosion. The loss of vegetative cover. Extinction. Desertification [steady advance of the desert]. Famine. The garbage crisis. . . .

Now, sometimes, developing countries feel the population argument is one made by wealthy countries who want to clamp down on their ability to grow. . . .

Let me answer that.

Sometimes the developing countries are right.

So I say this to citizens of the developed nations: we have a disproportionate impact on the global environment. We have less than a quarter of the world's population—but we use three quarters of the world's raw materials and create three quarters of all solid waste.

One way to put it is this: a child born in the United States will have thirty times more impact on the earth's environment during his or her lifetime than a child born in India.

The affluent [wealthy] of the world have a responsibility to deal with their disproportionate impact. . . .

Rapid population growth is only one of the causes of a profound transformation in the relationship between human civilization and the ecological system of the earth. . . .

Take, for example, the threat to our supply of fresh water.

There is a lot of water on earth. But there isn't very much fresh water—only about 2.5 percent of all water on earth is fresh and most of that is locked away as ice, say, in Antarctica, or Greenland, or other areas.

Furthermore, much of that water is used inefficiently. It also may be polluted by toxics and human waste. Meanwhile, by the year 2000, eighteen of the twenty-two largest metropolitan areas in the world—those with more than 10 million people—will be in developing countries. By 2025, 60 percent of the world's population will live in cities—that's more than 5 billion people. They will urgently need fresh water and water sanitation. . . .

What is the reason for the great popular indifference to these crises?

I sometimes like to remind people of the old science experiment involving a frog. Put the frog into a pot of boiling water and it jumps right out. It recognizes the danger.

But put the same frog into a pot of lukewarm water and bring it slowly to a boil. It'll just sit there until it is rescued (I've learned over the years that it's important to rescue the frog in the middle of the story).

The point of this story is that when the process of change seems gradual we have trouble recognizing it. From day to day, the lives of most of us seem not to change all that much. It is only when we lift our gaze beyond the next few days or years that we see the truth.

Similarly, even though our worldwide civilization confronts an unprecedented global environmental crisis, we can go from day to day without confronting the rapid change now underway. We must recognize the extent to which we are damaging the global environment, and we must develop new ways to work together. . . .

We can assume change is impossible. Or we can be part of the solution.

We can assume our enemies are too powerful—or we can assume the urgency of our mission is more powerful.

I believe there is every reason for hope. . . .

In the next few days, as we plan the future of this Commission, let us remember the spirit animating our meeting, thousands of miles to the South, exactly a year ago.

Remember how we achieved unity of purpose out of diversity. And let that memory of past success give us confidence that we will succeed in the future—and *for* the future.

≈≈≈≈≈≈≈≈≈≈≈≈≈≈≈≈≈≈≈≈≈≈≈≈≈≈≈≈≈≈≈≈≈≈≈≈≈≈

## THINKING CRITICALLY

1. What two environmental problems does Gore address?

2. What fault does Gore find with the environmental impact of developed countries?

3. What is the purpose of this speech? What impact, if any, did it have on you?

# Virginia Statute for Religious Freedom

In the years immediately following the American Revolution, the issue of the separation of church and state was the focus of much heated debate. The following measure, drafted by Thomas Jefferson, states that a person should have the right to follow his or her individual conscience, free from any influence or interference by the state, in matters related to religion. The Virginia Statute for Religious Freedom was adopted by the Virginia legislature in 1786 and served as the foundation on which the religion clauses in the U.S. Constitution and the Bill of Rights were based.

## I.

Well aware *that* Almighty God has created the mind free; *that* all attempts to influence it by temporal [civil] punishments or burdens or by civil incapacitations [lack of fitness for office], tend only to . . . [produce] habits of hypocrisy and meanness and are a departure from the plan of the Holy Author of our religion, who, being Lord both of body and mind, yet chose not to propagate [spread abroad] it by coercions [force] on either, as was in his Almighty power to do; *that* the impious [disrespectful] presumption of legislators and rulers, civil as well as ecclesiastical, who, being themselves but fallible and uninspired men, have assumed dominion [rule] over the faith of others, setting up their own opinions and modes [ways] of thinking as the only true and infallible [ones], and, as such, endeavoring to impose them on others, have established and maintained false religions over the greatest part of the world and through all time; *that* to compel a man to furnish contributions of money for the propagation [growth and spread] of opinions which he disbelieves is sinful and tyrannical; *that* even . . . forcing him to support this or that teacher of his own religious persuasion is depriving him of . . . comfortable liberty . . . *that* our civil rights have no dependence on our religious opinions any more than [on] our opinions in physics or geometry; *that* therefore the proscribing [of] any citizen as unworthy [of] the public confidence by laying upon him an incapacity of being called to offices of trust and emolument [payment for work] unless he profess or renounce this or that religious opinion is depriving him injuriously of those privileges and advantages to which in common with his fellow citizens he has a natural right; . . . *that* to suffer the civil magistrate to intrude his powers into the field of opinion . . . is a dangerous fallacy [falsehood] which at once destroys all religious liberty; . . . *that* it is time enough for the rightful purposes of civil government for its officers to interfere when principles break out into overt [open, or public] acts against peace and good order; and, finally, *that* truth is great and will prevail if left to herself, that she . . . has nothing to fear from the conflict, unless by human interposition [intrusion] disarmed of her natural weapons, free argument and debate. . . .

## II.

*Be it enacted by the General Assembly* that no man shall be compelled to frequent or support any religious worship, place, or ministry whatsoever, nor shall be enforced, restrained, molested, or burdened in his body or goods, nor shall otherwise suffer on account of his religious opinions or belief; but that all men shall be free to profess [state], and by argument to maintain, their opinion in matters of religion, and that the same shall in no wise diminish, enlarge, or affect their civil capacities.

## III.

And though we well know that this assembly, elected by the people for the ordinary purposes of legislation only, [has] no power to restrain the acts of succeeding assemblies, constituted [endowed] with powers equal to her own, and that therefore to declare this act to be irrevocable [not subject to change] would be of no effect in law; yet we are free to declare, and do declare, that the rights hereby asserted [strongly stated] are of the natural rights of mankind, and that if any act shall hereafter be passed to repeal the present or to narrow its operation, such act will be an infringement [violation] of natural right.

≈≈≈≈≈≈≈≈≈≈≈≈≈≈≈≈≈≈≈≈≈≈≈≈≈≈≈≈≈≈≈≈≈≈≈≈

## THINKING CRITICALLY

1. What does Jefferson say about taxation as related to religious freedom?
2. According to Jefferson, how does religious opinion relate to civil rights?
3. According to Jefferson, what are the natural weapons of humans? What is to be feared if these weapons are removed?

# Judiciary Act of 1789

The U.S. Constitution, which firmly established the powers and duties of Congress, is somewhat vague on issues relating to judicial power. Thus one of the first actions of the newly established First Congress was to establish a federal court system, one that could effectively balance the division of state versus federal power. Their decision, formalized in the Judiciary Act of 1789, was to establish a federal court system that could review and overturn decisions of state courts.

**S**ection 1. *Be it enacted* that the Supreme Court of the United States shall consist of a chief justice and five associate justices, any four of whom shall be a quorum and shall hold annually at the seat of government two sessions. . . . That the associate justices shall have precedence according to the date of their commissions, or when the commissions of two or more of them bear date on the same day according to their respective ages.

Section 2. *And be it further enacted*, that the United States shall be, and they hereby are, divided into thirteen districts. . . .

Section 3. *And be it further enacted*, that there be a court called a District Court in each of the aforementioned districts, to consist of one judge, who shall reside in the district for which he is appointed. . . .

Section 4. *And be it further enacted*, that the . . . districts . . . shall be divided into three circuits. . . . [T]hat there shall be held annually in each district of said circuits two courts, which shall be called circuit courts, and shall consist of any two justices of the Supreme Court and the district judge of such districts, any two of whom shall constitute a quorum. . . .

Section 9. *And be it further enacted*, that the district courts shall have, exclusively of the courts of the several states, cognizance [jurisdiction] of all crimes and offenses that shall be cognizable under the authority of the United States, committed within their respective districts or upon the high seas . . . and shall also have exclusive original cognizance of all civil cases of Admiralty and maritime jurisdiction. . . . And shall also have jurisdiction exclusively of the courts of the several States, of all suits against consuls or vice-consuls. . . . And the trial of issues in fact, in the district courts, in all cases except civil cases of Admiralty and maritime jurisdiction, shall be by jury. . . .

Section 11. *And be it further enacted*, that the circuit courts shall have original cognizance, concurrent with the courts of the several states, of all suits of a civil nature at common law or in equity, where the matter in dispute exceeds . . . $500, and the United States are plaintiffs or petitioners; or an alien is a party, or the suit is between a citizen of the state where the suit is brought and a citizen of another state. . . . And the circuit courts shall also have appellate jurisdiction from the district courts under the regulations and restrictions herinafter provided. . . .

Section 13. *And be it further enacted*, that the Supreme Court shall have exclusive jurisdiction of all controversies of a civil nature, where a state is a party, except between a state and its citizens; and except also between a state and citizens of other states, or aliens. . . . And shall have exclusively all such jurisdiction of suits or proceedings against ambassadors or other public ministers, or their domestics, or domestic servants, as a court of law can have or exercise consistently with the law of nations; and original, but not exclusive, jurisdiction of all suits brought by ambassadors or other public ministers, or in which a consul or vice-consul shall be a party. And the trial of issues in fact in the Supreme Court in all actions at law against citizens of the United States shall be by jury. The Supreme Court shall also have appellate jurisdiction from the circuit courts and courts of the several states in the cases hereinafter specially provided for . . . in cases warranted by the principle, and usages of law, to any courts appointed, or persons holding office under the authority of the United States. . . .

Section 25. *And be it further enacted*, that a final judgment or decree in any suit . . . where is drawn in question the validity of a treaty or statute of . . . the United States, and the decision is against their validity; or where is drawn in question the validity of a statute of . . . any state, on the ground of their being repugnant to the Constitution, treaties, or laws of the United States, and the decision is in favor of such their validity; or where is drawn in question the construction of any clause of the Constitution, or of a treaty, or statute of, or commission held under, the United States, and the decision is against the title, right, privilege, or exemption specially set up or claimed by either party, under such clause of the said Constitution, treaty, statute, or commission, may be reexamined, and reversed or affirmed in the Supreme Court of the United States upon a writ of error . . . and the writ shall have the same effect as if the judgment or decree complained of had been rendered or passed in a circuit court . . . except that the Supreme Court, instead of remanding [sending back] the case for a final decision as before provided, may, at their discretion, if the cause shall have been once remanded before, proceed to a final decision of the same and award execution. But no other error shall be assigned or regarded as a ground of reversal in any such case as aforesaid than such as appears on the face of the record, and immediately respects the beforementioned questions of validity or construction of the said Constitution, treaties, statutes, commissions, or authorities in dispute.

## THINKING CRITICALLY

1. Identify the organization and jurisdiction of the circuit courts.
2. Identify the jurisdiction of the Supreme Court.
3. What was the constitutional basis for Congress to establish a federal court system that could review and, if need be, overturn state court decisions?

# Dawes Act of 1887

In 1887, with the passage of the Dawes Act, Congress made the first attempt to bring the Native American population into mainstream American life. The act stated that the U.S. government would respond to Native Americans as groups rather than as individuals. Tribal leaders would no longer be able to speak for the community as a whole. In 1924 Congress finally extended U.S. citizenship to all Native Americans in the United States.

An act to provide for the allotment of lands in severalty [in one's own right] to Indians on the various reservations, and to extend the protection of the laws of the United States and the territories over the Indians, and for other purposes.

*Be it enacted:* That in all cases where any tribe or band of Indians has been, or shall hereafter be, located upon any reservation created for their use . . . the President of the United States . . . is authorized, whenever in his opinion any reservation . . . is advantageous for agriculture and grazing purposes, to cause said reservation . . . to be surveyed . . . and to allot the lands in said reservation in severalty to any Indian located thereon in quantities as follows:

To each head of a family, one-quarter of a section;

To each single person over eighteen years of age, one-eighth of a section;

To each orphan child under eighteen years of age, one-eighth of a section; and

To each other single person under eighteen years . . . one-sixteenth of a section. . . .

Section 5. That upon the approval of the allotments provided for in this act . . . the United States does and will hold the land thus allotted, for the period of twenty-five years, in trust for the sole use and benefit of the Indian to whom such allotment shall have been made . . . and that at the expiration of said period the United States will convey the same by patent [legal document] to said Indian, or his heirs . . . free of all charge. . . .

Section 6. That upon the completion of said allotments and the patenting of the lands to said allottees, each and every member of the respective bands or tribes of Indians to whom allotments have been made shall have the benefit of and be subject to the laws, both civil and criminal, of the state or territory in which they may reside. . . . And every Indian born within the territorial limits of the United States to whom allotments shall have been made under the provisions of this act, or under any law or treaty, and every Indian born within the territorial limits of the United States who has voluntarily taken up, within said limits, his residence separate and apart from any tribe of Indians therein, and has adopted the habits of civilized life, is hereby declared to be a citizen of the United States, and is entitled to all the rights, privileges, and immunities of such citizens.

## THINKING CRITICALLY

1. Identify the stated purpose of the Dawes Act.
2. Under what circumstances would an Indian be eligible for citizenship?
3. Why do you think some Native Americans would have resisted this act?

# Interstate Commerce Act of 1887

The Interstate Commerce Act, adopted by Congress in 1887, marked a turning point in the relationship between business and government. The act created the first regulatory commission in U.S. history and represented government's first attempt to reform the unfair business practices of the railroad industry.

*B*e *it enacted:* That the provisions of this act shall apply to any common carrier or common carriers engaged in the transportation of passengers or property wholly by railroad, or partly by railroad and partly by water when both are used. . . .

Section 2. That if any common carrier subject to the provisions of this act shall, directly or indirectly . . . charge, demand, collect, or receive from any person or persons a greater or less compensation for any service rendered . . . than it charges, demands, collects, or receives from any other person or persons for doing for him or them a like . . . service in the transportation of a like kind of traffic under substantially similar circumstances and conditions, such common carrier shall be deemed [considered] guilty of unjust discrimination, which is hereby prohibited and declared to be unlawful.

Section 3. That it shall be unlawful for any common carrier subject to the provisions of this act to make or give any undue or unreasonable preference or advantage to any particular person, company, firm, corporation, or locality. . . .

Section 4. That it shall be unlawful for any common carrier subject to the provisions of this act to charge or receive any greater compensation . . . for the transportation of passengers or of like kind of property, under substantially similar circumstances and conditions, for a shorter than for a longer distance over the same line, in the same direction, the shorter being included within the longer distance. . . .

Section 5. That it shall be unlawful for any common carrier subject to the provisions of this act to enter into any contract, agreement, or combination with any other common carrier or carriers for the pooling of freights of different and competing railroads. . . .

Section 6. That every common carrier subject to the provisions of this act shall print and keep for public inspection schedules showing the rates and fares and charges for the transportation of passengers and property. . . .

Section 11. That a Commission is hereby created and established to be known as the Interstate Commerce Commission.

## THINKING CRITICALLY

1. How does this act address the problem of discrimination?

2. Where in the act is the formation of monopolies addressed?

3. Some people believe that government interferes too much in the affairs of business. Do you agree or disagree with this view? Explain.

# Sherman Antitrust Act of 1890

The Sherman Antitrust Act of 1890 was the first federal legislation enacted to regulate the establishment and conduct of trusts. The act, which came in response to the creation of powerful trusts in major commodities such as steel, sugar, and beef, proved difficult to enforce. It did, however, pave the way for more effective antitrust legislation.

*B**e it enacted:*

Section 1. Every contract, combination in the form of trust or otherwise, or conspiracy, in restraint of trade or commerce among the several states, or with foreign nations, is hereby declared to be illegal. Every person who shall make any such contract or engage in any such combination or conspiracy, shall be deemed guilty of a misdemeanor. . . .

Section 2. Every person who shall monopolize, or attempt to monopolize . . . any part of the trade or commerce among the several states, or with foreign nations, shall be deemed guilty of a misdemeanor. . . .

Section 3. Every contract, combination in form of trust or otherwise, or conspiracy, in restraint of trade or commerce in any territory of the United States or of the District of Columbia, or . . . between any such territory and another, or between any such territory or territories and any state or states or the District of Columbia, or with foreign nations, or between the District of Columbia and any state or states or foreign nations, is hereby declared illegal. . . .

Section 4. The several circuit courts of the United States are hereby invested with jurisdiction [given the legal power] to prevent and restrain violations of this act. . . .

Section 5. Whenever it shall appear to the court . . . that the ends of justice require that other parties should be brought before the court, the court may cause them to be summoned. . . .

Section 6. Any property owned under any contract or by any combination, or pursuant to any conspiracy (and being the subject thereof) mentioned in section one of this act . . . shall be forfeited to the United States, and may be seized and condemned. . . .

Section 7. Any person who shall be injured in his business or property by any other person or corporation by reason of anything forbidden or declared to be unlawful by this act, may sue . . . without respect to the amount in controversy, and shall recover threefold the damages by him sustained. . . .

Section 8. That the word "person," or "persons," wherever used in this act shall be deemed to include corporations and associations.

## THINKING CRITICALLY

1. To whom does this act apply?
2. In what court's jurisdiction do violations of this act rest?
3. Why do you think this act would be difficult to enforce?

# Federal Reserve Act of 1913

In response to the Panic of 1907, brought about in part by the fact that the nation's monetary system had no means of increasing the amount of money in circulation, Congress in 1913 passed the Federal Reserve Act, thus creating a Federal Reserve Board, or the "Fed." The Fed became the central fixture in the execution of the nation's monetary policies.

*B*e it enacted . . . the Secretary of the Treasury, the Secretary of Agriculture and the Comptroller of the Currency . . . shall designate not less than eight nor more than twelve cities to be known as Federal reserve cities, and shall divide the continental United States, excluding Alaska, into districts, each district to contain only one of such Federal reserve cities. . . .

Section 3. Each Federal reserve bank shall establish branch banks within the Federal reserve district in which it is located and may do so in the district of any Federal reserve bank which may have been suspended. Such branches shall be operated by a board of directors under rules and regulations approved by the Federal Reserve Board. . . .

Section 5. The capital stock of each Federal reserve bank shall be divided into shares of $100 each. The outstanding capital stock shall be increased from time to time as member banks increase their capital stock and surplus or as additional banks become members, and may be decreased as member banks reduce their capital stock or surplus or cease to be members. . . .

Section 7. After all necessary expenses of a Federal reserve bank have been paid or provided for, the stockholders shall be entitled to receive an annual dividend of six per centum on the paid-in capital stock, which dividend shall be cumulative. After the aforesaid dividend claims have been fully met, all the net earnings shall be paid to the United States as a franchise tax, except that one-half of such net earnings shall be paid into a surplus fund until it shall amount to forty per centum of the paid-in capital stock of such bank.

The net earnings derived by the United States from Federal reserve banks shall, in the discretion of the Secretary, be used to supplement the gold reserve held against outstanding United States

notes, or shall be applied to the reduction of the outstanding bonded indebtedness of the United States under regulations to be prescribed by the Secretary of the Treasury. Should a Federal reserve bank be dissolved or go into liquidation, any surplus remaining, after the payment of all debts, dividend requirements as hereinbefore provided, and the par value of the stock, shall be paid to and become the property of the United States and shall be similarly applied. . . .

Section 10. A Federal Reserve Board is hereby created which shall consist of seven members, including the Secretary of the Treasury and the Comptroller of the Currency, who shall be members ex officio [by virtue of office], and five members appointed by the President of the United States, by and with the advice and consent of the Senate. In selecting the five appointive members of the Federal Reserve Board, not more than one of whom shall be selected from any one Federal reserve district, the President shall have due regard to a fair representation of the different commercial, industrial and geographical divisions of the country. The five members of the Federal Reserve Board appointed by the President and confirmed as aforesaid shall devote their entire time to the business of the Federal Reserve Board and shall each receive an annual salary of $12,000, payable monthly together with actual necessary traveling expenses, and the Comptroller of the Currency, as ex officio member of the Federal Reserve Board, shall, in addition to the salary now paid him as Comptroller of the Currency, receive the sum of $7,000 annually for his services as a member of said board. . . .

Section 13. Any Federal reserve bank may receive from any of its member banks, and from the United States, deposits of current funds in lawful money, national-bank notes, Federal reserve notes, or checks and drafts upon solvent member banks, payable upon presentation. . . .

[A]ny Federal reserve bank may discount notes, drafts, and bills of exchange arising out of actual commercial transactions; that is, notes, drafts, and bills of exchange issued or drawn for agricultural, industrial, or commercial purposes, or the proceeds of which have been used, or are to be used, for such purposes, the Federal Reserve Board to have the right to determine or define the character of the paper thus eligible for discount. . . .

Section 14. Any Federal reserve bank may, under rules and regulations prescribed by the Federal Reserve Board, purchase and sell in the open market, at home or abroad, either from or to domestic or foreign banks, firms, corporations, or individuals, cable transfers and bankers' acceptances and bills of exchange of the kinds and maturities by this Act made eligible for rediscount, with or without the indorsement of a member bank. . . .

Section 15. The moneys held in the general fund of the Treasury, except the five per centum fund for the redemption of outstanding national-bank notes and the funds provided in this Act for the redemption of Federal reserve notes may, upon the direction of the Secretary of the Treasury, be deposited in Federal reserve banks, which banks, when required by the Secretary of the Treasury, shall act as fiscal agents of the United States; and the revenues of the Government or any part thereof may be deposited in such banks, and disbursements may be made by checks drawn against such deposits. . . .

Section 16. Federal reserve notes, to be issued at the discretion of the Federal Reserve Board for the purpose of making advances to Federal reserve banks through the Federal reserve agents as hereinafter set forth and for no other purpose, are hereby authorized. The said notes shall be obligations of the United States and shall be receivable by all national and members banks and Federal reserve banks and for all taxes, customs, and other public dues. They shall be redeemed in gold on demand at the Treasury Department of the United States, in the city of Washington, District of Columbia, or in gold or lawful money at any Federal reserve bank.

≈≈≈≈≈≈≈≈≈≈≈≈≈≈≈≈≈≈≈≈≈≈≈≈≈≈≈≈≈≈≈≈≈≈≈≈≈

## THINKING CRITICALLY

1. For what purpose are the net earnings of the United States, as earned from the Federal reserve banks, to be used?

2. Where in the act is the Fed granted the power to make open-market operations?

3. Explain the significance of this act for the U.S. economy.

# Federal Trade Commission Act of 1914

A cornerstone of President Woodrow Wilson's "New Freedom" program was the passage of the Federal Trade Commission Act of 1914. By creating a Federal Trade Commission, Wilson hoped to put an end to monopolies and to establish a better understanding between big business and government.

*B*e it enacted . . . That a commission is hereby created and established, to be known as the Federal Trade Commission. . . .

Section 5. That unfair methods of competition in commerce are hereby declared unlawful.

The commission is hereby empowered and directed to prevent persons, partnerships, or corporations, except banks, and common carriers subject to the acts to regulate commerce, from using unfair methods of competition in commerce.

Whenever the commission shall have reason to believe that any such person, partnership, or corporation has been or is using any unfair method of competition in commerce, and if it shall appear to the commission that a proceeding by it in respect thereof would be to the interest of the public, it shall issue and serve upon such person, partnership, or corporation a complaint stating its charges in that respect, and containing a notice of a hearing upon a day and at a place therein fixed. . . .

Section 6. That the commission shall also have power:

(a) To gather and compile information concerning . . . any corporation engaged in commerce, excepting banks and common carriers . . . and its relation to other corporations and to individuals, associations, and partnerships.

(b) To require . . . corporations engaged in commerce . . . to file with the commission in such form as the commission may prescribe annual or special, or both annual and special, reports or answers in writing to specific questions, furnishing to the commission such information as it may require. . . .

(c) Whenever a final decree has been entered against any defendant corporation in any suit brought by the United States to prevent and restrain any violation of the antitrust acts . . . it shall be its duty to make such investigation. . . .

(d) Upon the direction of the President or either House of Congress to investigate and report the facts relating to any alleged violations of the antitrust acts by any corporation. . . .

(h) To investigate, from time to time, trade conditions in and with foreign countries where associations, combinations, or practices of manufacturers, merchants, or traders, or other conditions may affect the foreign trade of the United States, and to report to Congress thereon, with such recommendations as it deems advisable.

≈≈≈≈≈≈≈≈≈≈≈≈≈≈≈≈≈≈≈≈≈≈≈≈≈≈≈≈≈≈≈≈≈≈≈

## THINKING CRITICALLY

1. When can the Federal Trade Commission issue a complaint against a business?
2. To what types of businesses does this act *not* apply?
3. Whose interest is this act meant to protect? Provide specific examples from the excerpt to support your answer.

# Lend-Lease Act of 1941

In March 1941, nine months before the United States officially entered World War II, Congress passed and President Franklin D. Roosevelt approved the Lend-Lease Act. The act, for which Congress appropriated $7 billion, enabled any country whose defense the president deemed vital to that of the United States to receive the loan or lease of armaments and supplies.

*Be it enacted* . . . That this Act may be cited as "An Act to Promote the Defense of the United States". . . .

Section 3. (a) Notwithstanding the provisions of any other law, the President may, from time to time, when he deems it in the interest of national defense, authorize the Secretary of War, the Secretary of the Navy, or the head of any other department or agency of the Government—

(1) To manufacture in arsenals, factories, and shipyards under their jurisdiction, or otherwise procure . . . any defense article for the government of any country whose defense the President deems vital to the defense of the United States.

(2) To sell, transfer title to, exchange, lease, [or] lend . . . to any such government, any defense article. . . .

(3) To test, inspect, . . . or otherwise to place in good working order . . . any defense article for any such government. . . .

(b) The terms and conditions upon which any such foreign government receives any aid authorized under subsection (a) shall be those which the President deems satisfactory, and the benefit to the United States may be payment or repayment in kind [goods or commodities] or property, or any other direct or indirect benefit which the President deems satisfactory.

(c) After June 30, 1943, or after the passage of a concurrent resolution by the two Houses before June 30, 1943, which declares that the powers conferred by or pursuant [according] to subsection (a) are no longer necessary to promote the defense of the United States, neither the President nor the head of any department or agency shall exercise any of the powers conferred by or pursuant to subsection (a). . . .

Section 8. The Secretaries of War and of the Navy are hereby authorized to purchase or otherwise acquire arms . . . whenever the President deems such purchase or acquisition to be necessary in the interests of the defense of the United States.

Section 9. The President may, from time to time, promulgate [put into force] such rules and regulations as may be necessary and proper to carry out any of the provisions of this Act.

## THINKING CRITICALLY

1. Under the Lend-Lease Act, who has the power to authorize foreign aid?

2. Explain the provisions for ending the Lend-Lease program.

3. Notice that subsection (b) of the act does not specify when and how much countries will have to repay the United States for the aid they receive. Why do you think Congress and the president deliberately made this section of the act ambiguous?

# Civil Rights Act of 1964

In 1963 President John F. Kennedy sent a civil rights bill to the U.S. Congress. The bill was designed to end discrimination in public places, public education, and employment, and to secure equal voting rights. President Kennedy was assassinated before the landmark act was passed in 1964.

### Voting Rights

No person acting under color of law shall—in determining whether any individual is qualified under State law or laws to vote in any Federal election, apply any standard, practice, or procedure different from the standards, practices, or procedures applied under such law or laws to other individuals within the same county, parish, or similar political subdivision who have been found by State officials to be qualified to vote. . . .

### Discrimination in Places of Public Accommodation

All persons shall be entitled to the full and equal enjoyment of the goods, services, facilities, privileges, advantages, and accommodations of any place of public accommodation, as defined in this section without discrimination or segregation on the ground of race, color, religion, or national origin. . . .

### Desegregation of Public Education

Whenever the Attorney General receives a complaint in writing . . . and the Attorney General believes the complaint is meritorious [worthy] and certifies that the signer or signers of such complaint are unable, in his judgment, to initiate and maintain appropriate legal proceedings for relief and that the institution of an action will materially further the orderly achievement of desegregation in public education, the Attorney General is authorized, after giving notice of such complaint to the appropriate school board or college authority and after certifying that he is satisfied that such board or authority has had a reasonable time to adjust the conditions alleged [stated] in such complaint, to institute for or in the name of the United States a civil action in any appropriate district court of the United States against such parties and for such relief as may be appropriate. . . .

### Equal Employment Opportunity

It shall be an unlawful employment practice for an employer—to fail or refuse to hire or to discharge [fire] any individual, or otherwise to discriminate against any individual with respect to his compensation, terms, conditions, or privileges of employment, because of such individual's race, color, religion, sex, or national origin.

≈≈≈≈≈≈≈≈≈≈≈≈≈≈≈≈≈≈≈≈≈≈≈≈≈≈≈≈≈≈≈≈≈≈≈≈

## THINKING CRITICALLY

1. To what type of election does this act apply?
2. What must the attorney general do before instituting a civil action against a school board or college authority?
3. Why do you think this act is considered one of the most influential civil rights acts passed in U.S. history?

# Voting Rights Act of 1965

In March 1965, eight months after the Civil Rights Act brought the right of suffrage to people of all races and nationalities, discriminatory practices continued to prevent many people from voting. The Voting Rights Act of 1965 removed discriminatory barriers and extended the franchise to people of all educational and economic levels.

Section 4.  (a) To assure that the right of citizens of the United States to vote is not denied or abridged on account of race or color, no citizen shall be denied the right to vote in any Federal, State, or local election because of his failure to comply with any test or device in any State. . . .

(c) The phrase "test or device" shall mean any requirement that a person as a prerequisite for voting or registration for voting (1) demonstrate the ability to read, write, understand, or interpret any matter, (2) demonstrate any educational achievement or his knowledge of any particular subject, (3) possess good moral character, or (4) prove his qualifications by the voucher of registered voters or members of any other class. . . .

(e) (1) Congress hereby declares that to secure the rights under the fourteenth amendment of persons educated in American-flag schools in which the predominant classroom language was other than English, it is necessary to prohibit the States from conditioning the right to vote of such persons on ability to read, write, understand, or interpret any matter in the English language. . . .

Section 6.  Whenever . . . the Attorney General certifies . . . that (1) he has received complaints in writing from twenty or more residents of such political subdivision alleging [charging] that they have been denied the right to vote under color of law on account of race or color . . . or (2) that in his judgment . . . the appointment of examiners is otherwise necessary to enforce the guarantes of the fifteenth amendment, the Civil Service Commission shall appoint as many examiners for such subdivision as it may deem appropriate to prepare and maintain lists of persons eligible to vote in Federal, State, and local elections. . . .

Section 10.  (a)  The Congress finds that the requirement of the payment of a poll tax as a precondition to voting (i) precludes [prevents] persons of limited means from voting, or imposes unreasonable financial hardship upon such persons . . . , (ii) does not bear a reasonable relationship to any legitimate State interest in the conduct of elections, and (iii) in some areas has the purpose or effect of denying persons the right to vote because of race or color. Upon the basis of these findings, Congress declares that the constitutional right of citizens to vote is denied or abridged in some areas by the requirement of the payment of a poll tax as a precondition to voting.

## THINKING CRITICALLY

1. What educational standards does the act require as a prerequisite for voting?
2. According to the act, what are the problems with poll taxes?
3. Explain how poll taxes and testing requirements for voting are fundamentally undemocratic.

# Depository Institutions Deregulation Act of 1980

The Depository Institutions Deregulation Act of 1980 was designed to eliminate many of the differences that existed among financial institutions in the United States. The act forced U.S. banks to offer more competitive services and interest rates.

Section 202. (a) The Congress hereby finds that—

(1) limitations on the interest rates which are payable on deposits and accounts discourage persons from saving money, create inequities for depositors, impede [hinder] the ability of depository institutions to compete for funds, and have not achieved their purpose of providing an even flow of funds for home mortgage lending; and

(2) all depositors, and particularly those with modest savings, are entitled to receive a market rate of return on their savings as soon as it is economically feasible for depository institutions to pay such rate.

(b) It is the purpose of this title to provide for the orderly phase-out and the ultimate elimination of the limitations on the maximum rates of interest and dividends which may be paid on deposits and accounts by depository institutions by extending the authority to impose such limitations for 6 years, subject to specific standards designed to ensure a phase-out of such limitations to market rates of interest.

Section 203. (a) The authorities . . . to prescribe rules governing the payment of interest and dividends and the establishment of classes of deposits or accounts . . . are hereby transferred to the Depository Institutions Deregulation Committee (hereinafter in this title referred to as the "Deregulation Committee").

Section 204. (a) The Deregulation Committee shall, by regulation, exercise the authorities . . . to provide for the orderly phase-out and the ultimate elimination of the limitations on the maximum rates of interest and dividends which may be paid on deposits and accounts as rapidly as economic conditions warrant. . . .

(b) The Deregulation Committee shall work toward providing all depositors with a market rate of return on their savings with due regard for the safety and soundness of depository institutions. Pursuant to the authority granted by this title, the Deregulation Committee shall increase all limitations on the maximum rates of interest and dividends which may be paid on deposits and accounts to market rates as soon as feasible.

## THINKING CRITICALLY

1. What problems result from limitations on interest rates?
2. What are the goals of the Depository Institutions Deregulation Committee?
3. Who do you think felt the greatest benefits from this act?

# Americans with Disabilities Act of 1990

Passed by Congress in July of 1990, the Americans with Disabilities Act established a national commitment to the prohibition of discrimination based on disability. The act extended the equal protection laws afforded by the Civil Rights Act of 1964 to all Americans with disabilities.

**F**indings.—The Congress finds that—

(1) some 43,000,000 Americans have one or more physical or mental disabilities, and this number is increasing; . . .

(2) historically, society has tended to isolate and segregate individuals with disabilities; . . .

(3) discrimination against individuals with disabilities persists in such critical areas as employment, housing, public accommodations, education, transportation, communication, recreation, institutionalization, health services, voting, and access to public services;

(4) unlike individuals who have experienced discrimination on the basis of race, color, sex, national origin, religion, or age, individuals who have experienced discrimination on the basis of disability have often had no legal recourse to redress [correct] such discrimination;

(5) individuals with disabilities continually encounter various forms of discrimination, including . . . the discriminatory effects of architectural, transportation, and communication barriers, overprotective rules and policies, . . . segregation, and relegation to lesser services, programs, activities, benefits, jobs, or other opportunities;

(6) . . . studies have documented that people with disabilities, as a group, . . . are severely disadvantaged socially, vocationally, economically, and educationally; . . .

(8) the Nation's proper goals regarding individuals with disabilities are to assure equality of opportunity, full participation, independent living, and economic self-sufficiency; . . .

(9) the continuing existence of unfair and unnecessary discrimination and prejudice denies people with disabilities the opportunity to compete on an equal basis and to pursue those opportunities for which our free society is justifiably famous, and costs the United States billions of dollars in unnecessary expenses resulting from dependency and nonproductivity.

Purpose.—It is the purpose of this Act—

(1) to provide a clear and comprehensive national mandate for the elimination of discrimination against individuals with disabilities; . . .

(3) to ensure that the Federal Government plays a central role in enforcing the standards established in this Act on behalf of individuals with disabilities; and

(4) to invoke the sweep of congressional authority, including the power to enforce the fourteenth amendment and to regulate commerce, in order to address the major areas of discrimination faced day-to-day by people with disabilities.

## THINKING CRITICALLY

1. Prior to this act, how was discrimination on the basis of disability different from discrimination based on other factors?

2. How does discrimination on the basis of disability harm society as a whole?

3. Consider the accommodations for people with disabilities at your school. How do they help create a learning environment that is equally accessible to all students?

# Second Treatise of Civil Government

Englishman John Locke was one of the first political philosophers to challenge the divine rights of kings. His *Second Treatise of Civil Government*, which is excerpted here, was originally written in 1680 but was considered too radical to be published until 1690. It then became the philosophical basis for the theory that governmental authority must come only from the consent of the governed.

**M**an being born, as has been proved, with a title to perfect freedom, and an uncontrouled enjoyment of all the rights and privileges of the law of nature, equally with any other man, or number of men in the world, hath by nature a power, not only to preserve his property, that is, his life, liberty and estate, against the injuries and attempts of other men; but to judge of, and punish the breaches [violations] of that law in others, as he is persuaded the offence deserves, even with death itself, in crimes where the heinousness [horribleness] of the fact, in his opinion, requires it. But because no *political society* can be, nor subsist, without having in itself the power to preserve the property, and in order thereunto, punish the offences of all those of that society; there, and there only is *political society*, where every one of the members hath quitted this natural power, resigned it up into the hands of the community in all cases that exclude him not from appealing for protection to the law established by it. And thus all private judgment of every particular member being excluded, the community comes to be umpire, by settled standing rules, indifferent, and the same to all parties; and by men having authority from the community, for the execution of those rules, decides all the differences that may happen between any members of that society concerning any matter of right; and punishes those offences which any member hath committed against the society, with such penalties as the law has established: whereby it is easy to discern, who are, and who are not, in *political society* together. Those who are united into one body, and have a common established law and judicature [court system] to appeal to, with authority to decide controversies between them, and punish offenders, are in *civil society* one with another: but those who have no such common appeal, I mean on earth, are still in the state of nature, each being, where there is no other, judge for himself, and executioner; which is, as I have before shewed [shown] it, the perfect *state of nature.* . . .

Where-ever therefore any number of men are so united into one society, as to quit every one his executive power of the law of nature, and to resign it to the public, there and there only is a *political, or civil society.* And this is done, where-ever any number of men, in the state of nature, enter into society to make one people, one body politic, under one supreme government; or else when any one joins himself to, and incorporates with any government already made: for hereby he authorizes the society, or which is all one, the legislative thereof, to make laws for him, as the public good of the society shall require; to the execution whereof, his own assistance (as to his own decrees) is due. And this puts men out of a state of nature *into* that of a *common-wealth*, by setting up a judge on earth, with authority to determine all the controversies, and redress [remedy] the injuries that may happen to any member of the common-wealth; which judge is the legislative, or magistrates appointed by it. And where-ever there are any number of men, however associated, that have no such decisive power to appeal to, there they are still in *the state of nature.*

Hence it is evident, that *absolute monarchy*, which by some men is counted the only government in the world, is indeed *inconsistent with civil society*, and so can be no form of civil-government at all: for the *end of civil society*, being to avoid, and remedy those inconveniences of the state of nature, which necessarily follow from every man's being judge in his own case, by setting up a known authority, to which every one of that society may appeal upon any injury received, or controversy that may arise, and which every one of the society ought to obey; where-ever any persons are, who have not such an authority to appeal to, for the decision of any difference between them, there those persons are still *in the state of nature*; and so is every *absolute prince*, in respect of those who are under his *dominion*.

For he being supposed to have all, both legislative and executive power in himself alone, there is no judge to be found, no appeal lies open to any one, who may fairly, and indifferently, and with authority decide, and from whose decision relief and redress may be expected of any injury or inconviency, that may be suffered from the prince, or by his order: so that such a man, however intitled, *Czar*, or *Grand Seignor*, or however you please, is as much *in the state of nature*, with all under his dominion, as he is with the rest of mankind: for where-ever any two men are, who have no standing rule, and common judge to appeal to on earth, for the determination of controversies of right betwixt them, there they are still *in the state of nature*, and under all the inconveniences of it, with only this woful difference to the subject, or rather slave of an absolute prince: that whereas, in the ordinary state of nature, he has a liberty to judge of his right, and according to the best of his power, to maintain it; now, whenever his property is invaded by the will and order of his monarch, he has not only no appeal, as those in society ought to have, but as if he were degraded from the common state of rational creatures, is denied a liberty to judge of, or to defend his right; and so is exposed to all of the misery and inconveniencies, that a man can fear from one, who being in the unrestrained state of nature, is yet corrupted with flattery, and armed with power.

≈≈≈≈≈≈≈≈≈≈≈≈≈≈≈≈≈≈≈≈≈≈≈≈≈≈≈≈≈≈≈≈≈≈≈≈≈≈

## THINKING CRITICALLY

1. According to Locke, what must happen before people can achieve political society?

2. Why, according to Locke, is the absolute prince still in the state of nature?

3. What aspect of Locke's theory is paralleled in the American Declaration of Independence?

# The Social Contract

French philosopher Jean-Jacques Rousseau presented an idealized vision of the state of nature—a state of peace and equality in which the whole society agrees to be governed by the general will of all the people. His noted philosophical work *The Social Contract*, written in 1762 and excerpted here, became one of the leading influences in the French Revolution.

**M**an is born free, and everywhere he is in chains. He who believes himself the master of others does not escape being more of a slave than they. . . .

[S]ince men cannot engender [create] new forces, but merely unite and direct existing ones, they have no other means of maintaining themselves but to form by aggregation [joining together] a sum of forces that could gain the upper hand over the resistance, so that their forces are directed by means of a single moving power and made to act in concert.

This sum of forces cannot come into being without the cooperation of many. But since each man's force and liberty are the primary instruments of his maintenance, how is he going to engage them without hurting himself and without neglecting the care that he owes himself? This difficulty, seen in terms of my subject, can be stated in the following terms:

"Find a form of association which defends and protects with all common forces the person and goods of each associate, and by means of which each one, while uniting with all, nevertheless obeys only himself and remains as free as before?" This is the fundamental problem for which the social contract provides the solution.

The clauses of this contract are so determined by the nature of the act that the least modification renders them vain and ineffectual, that, although perhaps they have never been formally promulgated [declared], they are everywhere the same, everywhere tacitly [by nature] accepted and acknowledged. Once the social compact is violated, each person then regains his first rights and resumes his natural liberty, while losing the conventional liberty for which he renounced [abandoned] it.

These clauses, properly understood, are all reducible to a single one, namely the total alienation of each associate, together with all of his rights, to the entire community. For first of all, since each person gives himself whole and entire, the condition is equal for everyone; and since the condition is equal for everyone, no one has an interest in making it burdensome for the others.

Moreover, since the alienation is made without reservation, the union is as perfect as possible, and no associate has anything further to demand. For if some rights remained with private individuals, in the absence of any common superior who could decide between them and the public, each person would eventually claim to be his own judge in all things, since he is on some point his own judge. The state of nature would subsist and the association would become tyrannical or hollow.

Finally, in giving himself to all, each person gives himself to no one. And since there is no associate over whom he does not acquire the same right that he would grant others over himself, he gains the equivalent of everything he loses, along with a greater amount of force to preserve what he has.

If, therefore, one eliminates from the social compact whatever is not essential to it, one will find that it is reducible to the following terms. *Each of us places his person and all his power in common under the supreme direction of the general will; and as one we receive each member as an indivisible part of the whole.*

At once, in place of the individual person of each contracting party, this act of association produces a moral and collective body composed of as many members as there are voices in the assembly, which receives from this same act its unity, its common *self*, its life and its will. This public person, formed thus by union of all the others formerly took the name *city*, and at present takes the name *republic* or *body politic*, which is called *state* by its members when it is passive, *sovereign* when it is active, *power* when compared to others like itself. As to the associates, they collectively take the name *people*; individually they are called *citizens*, insofar as participants in the sovereign authority, and *subjects*, insofar as they are subjected to the laws of the state. . . .

This formula shows that the act of association includes a reciprocal [mutually dependent] commitment between the public and private individuals, and that each individual, contracting, as it were, with himself, finds himself under a twofold commitment: namely as a member of the sovereign to private individuals, and as a member of the state toward the sovereign. . . .

Thus, in order for the social compact to avoid being an empty formula, it tacitly entails the commitment—which alone can give force to the others—that whoever refuses to obey the general will will be forced to do so by the entire body. This means merely that he will be forced to be free. For this is the sort of condition that, by giving each citizen to the homeland, guarantees him against all personal dependence—a condition that produces the skill and the performance of the political machine, and which alone bestows legitimacy upon civil commitments. Without it such commitments would be absurd, tyrannical and subject to the worst abuses. . . .

What man loses through the social contract is his natural liberty and an unlimited right to everything that tempts him and that he can acquire. What he gains is civil liberty and the proprietary [exclusive] ownership of all he possesses. So as not to be in error in these compensations, it is necessary to draw a careful distinction between natural liberty (which is limited solely by the force of the individual involved) and civil liberty (which is limited by the general will), and between possession (which is merely the effect of the force or the right of the first occupant) and proprietary ownership (which is based solely on a positive title).

≈≈≈≈≈≈≈≈≈≈≈≈≈≈≈≈≈≈≈≈≈≈≈≈≈≈≈≈≈≈≈≈≈≈

## THINKING CRITICALLY

1. According to Rousseau, why does a person remain free when he or she enters into political association with others?

2. What do people gain and lose as a result of entering into the social contract?

3. According to Rousseau, how does the person who enters into the social contract perceive all of the people who have also entered into it? Do you agree with this assumption? Explain.

# *The Wealth of Nations*

Scottish economist Adam Smith first described his theory of the "invisible hand" in his 1776 book *The Wealth of Nations.* Since that time, the "invisible hand" has become the basis of the concept of the free market. In the following excerpt from his book, Smith explains his rationale for keeping domestic markets open to foreign competition.

The general industry of the society never can exceed what the capital of the society can employ. As the number of workmen that can be kept in employment by any particular person must bear a certain proportion to his capital, so the number of those than can be continually employed by all the members of a great society, must bear a certain proportion to the whole capital of that society, and never can exceed that proportion. No regulation of commerce can increase the quantity of industry in any society beyond what its capital can maintain. It can only divert a part of it into a direction into which it might not otherwise have gone; and it is by no means certain that this artificial direction is likely to be more advantageous to the society than that into which it would have gone of its own accord.

Every individual is continually exerting himself to find out the most advantageous employment for whatever capital he can command. It is his own advantage, indeed, and not that of the society, which he has in view. But the study of his own advantage naturally, or rather necessarily leads him to prefer that employment which is most advantageous to the society.

First, every individual endeavours to employ his capital as near home as he can, and consequently as much as he can in the support of domestic industry; provided always that he can thereby obtain the ordinary, or not a great deal less than the ordinary profits of stock. . . .

Secondly, every individual who employs his capital in the support of domestic industry, necessarily endeavours so to direct that industry, that its produce may be of the greatest possible value.

The produce of industry is what it adds to the subject or materials upon which it is employed. In proportion as the value of this produce is great or small, so will likewise be the profits of the employer. But it is only for the sake of profit that any man employs a capital in the support of industry; and he will always, therefore, endeavour to employ it in the support of that industry of which the produce is likely to be of the greatest value, or to exchange for the greatest quantity either of money or of other goods.

But the annual revenue of every society is always precisely equal to the exchangeable value of the whole annual produce of its industry, or rather is precisely the same thing with that exchangeable value. As every individual, therefore, endeavours as much as he can both to employ his capital in the support of domestic industry, and so to direct that industry that its produce may be of the greatest value; every individual necessarily labours to render the annual revenue of the society as great as he can. He generally, indeed, neither intends to promote the public interest, nor knows how much he is promoting it. By preferring the support of domestic to that of foreign industry, he intends only his own security; and by directing that industry in such a manner as its produce may be of the greatest value, he intends only his own gain, and he is in this, as in many other cases, led by an invisible hand to promote an end which was no part of his intention. Nor is it always the worse for society that it was no part of it. By pursuing his own interest he frequently promotes that of the society more effectually [effectively] than when he really intends to promote it. I have never known much good done by those who affected [pretended] to trade for the public good. It is an affectation [a pretense], indeed, not very common among merchants, and very few words need be employed in dissuading [deterring] them from it.

What is the species of domestic industry which his capital can employ, and of which the produce is likely to be of the greatest value, every individual, it is evident, can, in his local situation, judge much better than any statesman or lawgiver can do for him. The statesman, who should attempt to direct private people in what manner they ought to employ their capitals, would not only load himself with a most unnecessary attention, but assume an authority which could safely be trusted, not only to no single person, but to no council or senate whatever, and which would nowhere be so dangerous as in the hands of a man who had folly and presumption enough to fancy [consider] himself fit to exercise it.

To give the monopoly of the home-market to the produce of domestic industry, in any particular art or manufacture, is in some measure to direct private people in what manner they ought to employ their capitals, and must, in almost all cases, be either a useless or a hurtful regulation. If the produce of domestic can be brought there as cheap as that of foreign industry, the regulation is evidently useless. If it cannot, it must generally be hurtful. It is the maxim of every prudent master of a family, never to attempt to make at home what it will cost him more to make than to buy. The taylor does not attempt to make his own shoes, but buys them from a shoemaker. The shoemaker does not attempt to make his own clothes, but employs a taylor. The farmer attempts to make neither the one not the other, but employs those different artificers [craftspeople]. All of them find it for their interest to employ their whole industry in a way in which they have some advantage over their neighbours, and to purchase with a part of its produce, or what is the same thing, with the price of a part of it, whatever else they have occasion for [need].

What is prudence in the conduct of every private family, can scarce be folly in that of a great kingdom. If a foreign country can supply us with a commodity cheaper than we ourselves can make it, better buy it of them with some part of the produce of our own industry, employed in a way in which we have some advantage.

≈≈≈≈≈≈≈≈≈≈≈≈≈≈≈≈≈≈≈≈≈≈≈≈≈≈≈≈≈≈≈≈≈≈≈≈≈

## THINKING CRITICALLY

1. According to Smith, what determines the size of a society's industry?
2. Explain Smith's theory of the "invisible hand."
3. Do you agree that markets will naturally evolve fairly and profitably without the intervention of the government, or do you think government intervention is necessary to promote and monitor business? Explain.

# *Common Sense*

The first clear call for American independence was voiced by Thomas Paine in his 1776 pamphlet, *Common Sense*. Written at a time when most people in the colonies were only debating the possibility of self-government, the pamphlet served to solidify the belief among colonists that the time was right to revolt against British domination. So powerful was the message contained in *Common Sense*, excerpted here, that within only a few months after its publication, thousands of copies had been circulated in the American colonies and four editions had been published in Europe.

In the following pages I offer nothing more than simple facts, plain arguments, and common sense; and have no other preliminaries to settle with [suggest to] the reader than that he will divest [strip] himself of prejudice and prepossession [bias], and suffer [allow] his reason and his feelings to determine for themselves; that he will put on, or rather that he will not put off, the true character of a man, and generously enlarge his views beyond the present day.

Volumes have been written on the subject of the struggle between England and America. Men of all ranks have embarked in the controversy, from different motives and with various designs; but all have been ineffectual, and the period of debate is closed. Arms as the last resource decide the contest; the appeal was the choice of the king, and the continent has accepted the challenge. . . .

The sun never shined on a cause of greater worth. 'Tis not the affair of a city, a county, a province, or a kingdom, but of a continent—of at least one-eighth part of a habitable globe. 'Tis not the concern of a day, a year, or an age; posterity [future generations] are virtually involved in the contest, and will be more or less affected even to the end of time by the proceedings now. Now is the seed-time of continental union, faith, and honor. The least fracture now will be like a name engraved with the point of a pin on the tender rind of a young oak; the wound would enlarge with the tree, and posterity read it in full-grown characters. . . .

I have heard it asserted by some that, as America has flourished under her former connection with Great Britain, the same connection is necessary toward her future happiness and will always have the same effect. Nothing can be more falla-

cious than this kind of argument. We may as well assert that because a child has thrived upon milk that it is never to have meat, or that the first twenty years of our lives is to become a precedent for the next twenty. But even this is admitting more than is true; for I answer roundly that America would have flourished as much, and probably much more, had no European power had anything to do with her. The commerce by which she has enriched herself are the necessaries of life and will always have a market while eating is the custom of Europe. . . .

But Britain is the parent country, say some. Then the more shame upon her conduct. Even brutes do not devour their young nor savages make war upon their families. . . . Europe, and not England, is the parent country of America. This New World has been the asylum for the persecuted lovers of civil and religious liberty from *every part* of Europe. Hither have they fled, not from the tender embraces of the mother, but from the cruelty of the monster; and it is so far true of England that the same tyranny which drove the first emigrants from home pursues their descendants still. . . .

I challenge the warmest advocate for reconciliation to show a single advantage that this continent can reap by being connected with Great Britain. I repeat the challenge; not a single advantage is derived. Our corn will fetch its price in any market in Europe, and our imported goods must be paid for, buy them where we will.

But the injuries and disadvantages we sustain by that connection are without number, and our duty to mankind at large, as well as to ourselves, instruct us to renounce [abandon] the alliance; because any submission to or dependence on Great Britain tends directly to involve this continent in European wars and quarrels and sets us at variance with nations who would otherwise seek our friendship and against whom we have neither anger nor complaint. As Europe is our market for trade, we ought to form no partial [biased] connection with any part of it. . . .

Everything that is right or natural pleads for separation. The blood of the slain, the weeping voice of nature cries, "*'Tis time to part.*" Even the distance at which the Almighty has placed England and America is a strong and natural proof that the authority of the one over the other was never the design of heaven. . . .

The authority of Great Britain over this continent is a form of government which sooner or later must have an end. And a serious mind can draw no true pleasure by looking forward, under the painful and positive conviction that what he calls "the present constitution" is merely temporary. . . .

But where, says some, is the king of America? I'll tell you, friend, he reigns above, and does not make havoc of mankind like the royal brute of Britain . . . in America *the law is king.* For as in absolute governments the king is law, so in free countries the law *ought* to be king. . . .

A government of our own is our natural right; and when a man seriously reflects on the precariousness of human affairs, he will become convinced that it is infinitely wiser and safer to form a Constitution of our own in a cool, deliberate manner while we have it in our power than to trust such an interesting event to time and chance. . . .

Our present condition is legislation without law, wisdom without a plan, a constitution without a name, and, what is strangely astonishing, perfect independence contending for dependence. . . .

We ought to reflect that there are three different ways by which an independence may hereafter be effected; and that *one* of those *three* will, one day or other, be the fate of America, viz., by the legal voice of the people in Congress, by a military power, or by a mob. . . . Should an independence be brought about by the first of those means, we have every opportunity and every encouragement before us to form the noblest, purest constitution on the face of the earth. . . .

On these grounds I rest the matter . . . let none other be heard among us than those of a *good citizen, an open and resolute friend, and a virtuous supporter of the rights of mankind and of the free and independent states of America.*

≈≈≈≈≈≈≈≈≈≈≈≈≈≈≈≈≈≈≈≈≈≈≈≈≈≈≈≈≈≈≈≈≈≈≈

## THINKING CRITICALLY

1. Why does Paine say that Europe, not England, is the parent country of America?
2. What argument does Paine give for abandoning the alliance with Great Britain?
3. Why do you think Paine's pamphlet was so successful?

# "The Federalist, Number 10"

The best-known arguments in the debate over the ratification of the Constitution of the United States appeared in a collection of 85 essays known as *The Federalist Papers*. The most famous of these essays, "The Federalist, Number 10," written by James Madison, addressed Antifederalists' concerns that the United States had too many small groups, or "factions," to be governed democratically by a single government. Madison, acknowledging the presence of factions, argued that majority rule should be the central governing concern and that protection of the majority may sometimes come at the expense of minority rights.

Among the numerous advantages promised by a well-constructed union, none deserves to be more accurately developed than its tendency to break and control the violence of faction. The friend of popular governments never finds himself so much alarmed for their character and fate as when he contemplates their propensity [inclination] to this dangerous vice. . . .

By a faction, I understand a number of citizens, whether amounting to a majority or minority of the whole, who are united and actuated [moved] by some common impulse of passion, or of interest, adverse [opposed] to the rights of other citizens or to the permanent and aggregate [collective] interests of the community.

There are two methods of curing the mischiefs of faction: the one, by removing its causes; the other, by controlling its effects.

There are again two methods of removing the causes of faction: the one, by destroying the liberty which is essential to its existence; the other, by giving to every citizen the same opinions, the same passions, and the same interests.

It could never be more truly said than of the first remedy, that it was worse than the disease. Liberty is to faction what air is to fire, an ailment without which it instantly expires. But it could not be less folly to abolish liberty, which is essential to political life, because it nourishes faction, than it would be to wish the annihilation of air, which is essential to animal life, because it imparts to fire its destructive agency.

The second expedient is as impracticable as the first would be unwise. As long as the reason of man continues fallible [capable of error], and he is at liberty to exercise it, different opinions will be formed. As long as the connection subsists [persists] between his reason and his self-love, his opinions and his passions will have a reciprocal [mutually dependent] influence on each other. . . .

The inference to which we are brought is that the causes of faction cannot be removed, and that relief is only to be sought in the means of controlling its effects.

If a faction consists of less than a majority, relief is supplied by the republican principle, which enables the majority to defeat its sinister views by regular vote. It may clog the administration, it may convulse [shake up] the society; but it will be unable to execute and mask its violence under the forms of the Constitution. When a majority is included in a faction, the form of popular government, on the other hand, enables it to sacrifice to its ruling passion or interest both the public good and the rights of other citizens. To secure the public good, and private rights, against the danger of such a faction, and at the same time to preserve the spirit and the form of popular government, is then the great object to which our inquiries are directed. Let me add that it is the great *desideratum* [desired objective] by which alone this form of government can be rescued from the opprobrium [disgrace] under which it has so long labored, and be recommended to the esteem and adoption of mankind.

## THINKING CRITICALLY

1. In your own words, define the term *faction*.
2. Why, according to Madison, can the causes of factions not be removed?
3. Do you think that, in today's society, factions and interest groups hurt or help society? Provide an example.

# "The Federalist, Number 71"

During the debate over the ratification of the U.S. Constitution, issues relating to the establishment of the new government were fiercely contested. The most powerful arguments in support of the Constitution were included in a compilation of 85 essays known as *The Federalist Papers*. In "The Federalist, Number 71," Alexander Hamilton argues for a four-year term of office for the president.

**D**uration in office has been mentioned as the second requisite to the energy of the Executive authority [president]. . . . It is a general principle of human nature, that a man will be interested in whatever he possesses, in proportion to the firmness or precariousness of the tenure by which he holds it; [and] will be less attached to what he holds by a momentary or uncertain title than to what he enjoys by a durable or certain title. . . . [A] man acting in the capacity of chief magistrate under a consciousness that in a very short time he *must* lay down his office, will be apt to feel himself too little interested in it to hazard any material censure or perplexity. . . . If the case should only be that he *might* lay it down . . . his wishes, conspiring with his fears, would tend still more powerfully to corrupt his integrity, or debase [lessen] his fortitude [courage]. In either case, feebleness and irresolution [hesitation] must be the characteristics of the station. . . .

But however inclined we might be to insist upon an unbounded complaisance [agreeableness] in the Executive to the inclinations of the people, we can with no propriety contend for a like complaisance to the humors of the legislature. . . . [I]t is certainly desirable that the Executive should be in a situation to dare to act his own opinion with vigor and decision. . . .

It may perhaps be asked how the shortness of the duration in office can affect the independence of the Executive on the legislature, unless the one were possessed of the power of appointing or displacing the other. One answer [is] the little inducement [incentive] it affords him to expose himself, on account of it, to any considerable inconvenience or hazard. Another answer . . . will result from the consideration of the influence of the legislative body over the people; which might be employed to prevent the reelection of a man who, by an upright resistance to any sinister project of that body, should have made himself obnoxious to its resentment. . . .

It cannot be affirmed that a duration of four years, or any other limited duration, would completely answer the end proposed; but it would contribute towards it in a degree which would have a material influence upon the spirit and character of the government.

≈≈≈≈≈≈≈≈≈≈≈≈≈≈≈≈≈≈≈≈≈≈≈≈≈≈≈≈≈≈≈≈≈

## THINKING CRITICALLY

1. According to Hamilton, what is to be feared if the president's length of time in office is too short?

2. What impact does length of time in office have on the relationship between the president and the legislature?

3. Do you think that the four-year term of the presidency is an appropriate duration? Explain.

# *Elements of Political Economy*

In the following excerpt from *Elements of Political Economy*, originally published in 1821, Scottish economist James Mill discusses the cause-and-effect relationship between supply and demand. More specifically, Mill seeks to answer the question of what determines the quantity in which commodities will exchange for one another.

When a certain quantity of one commodity is exchanged for a certain quantity of another commodity; a certain quantity of cloth, for example, for a certain quantity of corn; there is something which determines the owner of the cloth to accept for it such and such a quantity of corn; and, in like manner, the owner of the corn to accept such and such a quantity of cloth.

This is, evidently, the principle of demand and supply. . . . If a great quantity of corn comes to market to be exchanged for cloth, and only a small quantity of cloth to be exchanged for corn, a great quantity of corn will be given for a small quantity of cloth. If the quantity of cloth, which thus comes to market, is increased, without any increase in the quantity of corn, the quantity of corn which is exchanged for a given quantity of cloth will be proportionately diminished. . . .

Demand creates, and the loss of demand annihilates [destroys], supply. When an increased demand arises for any commodity, an increase of supply, if the supply is capable of increase, follows, as a regular effect. If the demand for any commodity altogether ceases, the commodity is no longer produced.

The connexion here, of causes and effects, is easily explained. If corn is brought to market, the cost of bringing it has been so much. If cloth is brought to market, the cost of bringing it to market has been so much. . . .

The cost of bringing the corn to market has either been equal to that of bringing the cloth, or unequal. If it has been equal, there is no motive, to those who bring the cloth or the corn, for altering the quantity of either. They cannot obtain more of the commodity which they receive in exchange, by transferring their labour to its production. If the cost has been unequal, there immediately arises a motive for altering the proportions. Suppose that the cost of bringing the whole of the corn has been greater than that of bringing the whole of the cloth; and that the whole of the one is exchanged against the whole of the other, either at once, or in parts; the persons who brought the cloth have in that case possessed themselves of a quantity of corn at less cost, than that at which it was brought to market, by those who produced it; those, on the other hand, who brought the corn have possessed themselves of a quantity of cloth, at a greater cost than that at which it can be made and brought to market.

## THINKING CRITICALLY

1. What happens if the supply of one commodity is much greater than the supply of another commodity?

2. How does the demand for a commodity affect the supply of that commodity?

3. Using Mill's example of the cloth and the corn, provide a scenario that might cause the cost of corn to be extremely high. What would cause it to be high, and how would the price of cloth be affected?

# *Democracy in America*

In 1831 French writer and politician Alexis de Tocqueville traveled to the United States to gain a firsthand view of the young nation, its institutions, and its people. In 1835 he published *Democracy in America*, a perceptive analysis of the social structure and political system of the United States. In the following excerpt from his book, de Tocqueville discusses the importance of the township in the American political structure of the early nineteenth century.

It is proposed to examine in the following chapter what is the form of government established in America on the principle of the sovereignty of the people; what are its resources, its hindrances, its advantages, and its dangers. . . .

It is not undesignedly that I begin this subject with the township. The village or township is the only association which is so perfectly natural that wherever a number of men are collected it seems to constitute itself.

The town, or tithing, as the smallest division of a community, must necessarily exist in all nations, whatever their laws or customs may be. . . . A nation is always able to establish great political assemblies, because it habitually contains a certain number of individuals fitted by their talents, if not by their habits, for the direction of affairs. The township is, on the contrary, comprised of coarser materials, which are less easily fashioned by the legislator. The difficulties which attend the consolidation of its independence rather augment [enhance] than diminish with the increasing enlightenment of the people. . . . Again, no immunities are so ill protected from the encroachments [infringements] of the supreme power as those of municipal bodies in general: they are unable to struggle, single-handed, against a strong or an enterprising government, and they cannot defend their cause with success unless it be identified with the customs of the nation and supported by public opinion. Thus, until the independence of townships is amalgamated [incorporated into] with the manners of a people it is easily destroyed, and it is only after a long existence in the laws that it can be thus amalgamated. . . . Nevertheless local assemblies of citizens constitute the strength of free nations. Town meetings are to liberty what primary schools are to science; they bring it within the people's reach, they teach men how to use and how to enjoy it. A nation may establish a system of free government, but without the spirit of municipal institutions it cannot have the spirit of liberty. The transient [temporary] passions and the interests of an hour, or the chance of circumstances, may have created the external forms of independence; but the despotic [totalitarian] tendency which has been repelled will, sooner or later, inevitably reappear on the surface.

## THINKING CRITICALLY

1. Why are nations able to form great political assemblies?
2. According to de Tocqueville, how are towns the strength of free nations?
3. Do you think that de Tocqueville's assessment of the importance of townships holds true in U.S. society today? Explain.

# "Civil Disobedience"

Poet and essayist Henry David Thoreau was one of the most noted Transcendentalist thinkers in U.S. history. In support of his antislavery beliefs, he refused to pay a Massachusetts poll tax during the Mexican War because he regarded the war as a means to extend slavery. For this action, Thoreau was arrested and jailed. In 1849 he related his experiences in the influential political essay "Civil Disobedience." The essay became one of the leading works in the passive resistance movement.

I heartily accept the motto, "That government is best which governs least"; and I should like to see it acted up to more rapidly and systematically. Carried out, it finally amounts to this, which also I believe,—"That government is best which governs not at all"; and when men are prepared for it, that will be the kind of government which they will have. Government is at best but an expedient [a means to an end]; but most governments are usually, and all governments are sometimes, inexpedient. . . . Witness the present Mexican war, the work of comparatively a few individuals using the standing government as their tool; for, in the outset, the people would not have consented to this measure.

This American government,—what is it but a tradition, though a recent one, endeavoring to transmit itself unimpaired to posterity [future generations], but each instant losing some of its integrity? It has not the vitality and force of a single living man; for a single man can bend it to his will. It is a sort of wooden gun to the people themselves. But it is not the less necessary for this; for the people must have some complicated machinery or other, and hear its din [clamor], to satisfy that idea of government which they have. Governments show thus how successfully men can be imposed on, even impose on themselves, for their own advantage. It is excellent, we must all allow. Yet this government never of itself furthered any enterprise, but by the alacrity [quickness] with which it got out of its way. It does not keep the country free. It does not settle the West. It does not educate. The character inherent in the American people has done all that has been accomplished; and it would have done somewhat more, if the government had not sometimes got in its way. . . .

But, to speak practically and as a citizen, unlike those who call themselves no-government men, I ask for, not at once no government, but at once a better government. Let every man make known what kind of government would command his respect, and that will be one step toward obtaining it. . . .

Can there not be a government in which majorities do not virtually decide right and wrong, but conscience?—in which majorities decide only those questions to which the rule of expediency is applicable? Must the citizen ever for a moment, or in the least degree, resign his conscience to the legislator? Why has every man a conscience, then? I think that we should be men first, and subjects afterward. It is not desirable to cultivate a respect for the law, so much as for the right. The only obligation which I have a right to assume is to do at any time what I think right. . . .

How can a man be satisfied to entertain an opinion merely, and enjoy it? Is there any enjoyment in it, if his opinion is that he is aggrieved? If you are cheated out of a single dollar by your neighbor, you do not rest satisfied with knowing that you are cheated, or with saying that you are cheated, or even with petitioning him to pay you your due; but you take effectual steps at once to obtain the full amount, and see that you are never cheated again. . . .

Unjust laws exist: shall we be content to obey them, or shall we endeavor to amend them, and obey them until we have succeeded, or shall we transgress [disobey] them at once? Men generally, under such a government as this, think that they ought to wait until they have persuaded the majority to alter them. They think that, if they should resist, the remedy would be worse than the evil. But it is the fault of the government itself that the remedy is worse than the evil. It makes it worse. Why is it not more apt to anticipate and provide for reform? Why does it not cherish its wise minority? Why does it cry and resist before it is hurt? Why does it not encourage its citizens to be on the alert to point out its faults, and do better than it would have them? . . .

One would think, that a deliberate and practical denial of its authority was the only offence never contemplated by government; else, why has it not assigned its definite, its suitable and proportionate, penalty? If a man who has no property refuses but once to earn nine shillings for the State, he is put in prison for a period unlimited by any law that I know, and determined only by the discretion of those who placed him there; but if he should steal ninety times nine shillings from the State, he is soon permitted to go at large again.

If the injustice is part of the necessary friction [workings] of the machine of government, let it go, let it go: perchance [perhaps] it will wear smooth—certainly the machine will wear out. If the injustice has a spring, or a pulley, or a rope, or a crank, exclusively for itself, then perhaps you may consider whether the remedy will not be worse than the evil; but if it is of such a nature that it requires you to be the agent of injustice to another, then I say, break the law.

## THINKING CRITICALLY

1. According to Thoreau, who is responsible for the success of the United States? What entity has kept it from achieving more?

2. Under what circumstances does Thoreau believe it is appropriate to break the law?

3. What assumption does Thoreau make about the integrity of human character? Do you agree with this assumption and, based on this, what type of society do you think would result from the type of behavior Thoreau is suggesting?

# *On Liberty*

In his book *On Liberty*, political theorist John Stuart Mill advanced the argument that certain freedoms should not be limited in a democratic society. In the following excerpt from his book, which was written in 1859, Mill explains the dangers in suppressing an individual's freedom to express his or her opinions.

If all mankind minus one, were of one opinion, and only one person were of the contrary opinion, mankind would be no more justified in silencing that one person, than he, if he had the power, would be justified in silencing mankind. Were an opinion a personal possession of no value except to the owner; if to be obstructed in the enjoyment of it were simply a private injury, it would make some difference whether the injury was inflicted only on a few persons or on many. But the peculiar evil of silencing the expression of an opinion is, that it is robbing the human race, posterity as well as the existing generation; those whose dissent from the opinion, still more than those who hold it. If the opinion is right, they are deprived of the opportunity of exchanging error for truth: if wrong, they lose, what is almost as great a benefit, the clearer perception and livelier impression of truth, produced by its collision with error. . . .

We can never be sure that the opinion we are endeavouring to stifle is a false opinion; and if we were sure, stifling it would be an evil still.

First: the opinion which it is attempted to suppress by authority may possibly be true. Those who desire to suppress it, of course deny its truth; but they are not infallible [incapable of error]. They have no authority to decide the question for all mankind, and exclude every other person from the means of judging. To refuse a hearing to an opinion, because they are sure that it is false, is to assume that *their* certainty is the same thing as *absolute* certainty. All silencing of discussion is an assumption of infallibility. . . .

Men, and governments, must act to the best of their ability. There is no such thing as absolute certainty, but there is assurance sufficient for the purposes of human life. We may, and must, assume our opinion to be true for the guidance of our own conduct: and it is assuming no more when we for-

bid bad men to pervert society by the propagation [growth and spread] of opinions which we regard as false and pernicious [harmful].

I answer, that it is assuming very much more. There is the greatest difference between presuming an opinion to be true, because, with every opportunity for contesting it, it has not been refuted, and assuming its truth for the purpose of not permitting its refutation. Complete liberty of contradicting and disproving our opinion, is the very condition which justifies us in assuming its truth for purposes of action; and on no other terms can a being with human faculties have any rational assurance of being right. . . .

We have now recognized the necessity to the mental well-being of mankind (on which all their other well-being depends) of freedom of opinion, and freedom of the expression of opinion, on four distinct grounds; which we will now briefly recapitulate [summarize].

First, if any opinion is compelled to silence, that opinion may . . . be true. To deny this is to assume our own infallibility.

Secondly, though the silenced opinion be an error, it may, and very commonly does, contain a portion of truth; and since the general or prevailing opinion on any subject is rarely or never the whole truth, it is only by the collision of adverse opinions that the remainder of the truth has any chance of being supplied.

Thirdly, even if the received opinion be not only true, but the whole truth; unless it is suffered to be, and actually is, vigorously and earnestly contested, it will, by most of those who receive it, be held in the manner of a prejudice, with little comprehension of feeling of its rational grounds. And not only this, but, fourthly the meaning of the doctrine itself will be in danger of being lost, or enfeebled, and deprived of its vital effect on the character and conduct: the dogma becoming a mere formal profession . . . and preventing the growth of any real and heartfelt conviction from reason or personal experience.

≈≈≈≈≈≈≈≈≈≈≈≈≈≈≈≈≈≈≈≈≈≈≈≈≈≈≈≈≈≈≈≈

## THINKING CRITICALLY

1. According to Mill, what is to be feared when the freedom of expression of opinion is denied?

2. According to Mill, how does a person prove that his or her opinion is right?

3. Do you believe that people should always have the freedom to express their opinions? Why or why not?

# *Das Kapital*

In *Das Kapital*, which became the handbook for socialist economies, Karl Marx and Friedrich Engels presented a critical assessment of capitalist economic structures. In the following excerpt, from the introductory chapter on commodities, the authors discuss the difference between a commodity's relative value and its intrinsic value, or use-value.

The wealth of those societies in which the capitalist mode of production prevails, presents itself as "an immense accumulation of commodities," its unit being a single commodity. Our investigation must therefore begin with the analysis of a commodity.

A commodity is, in the first place, an object outside us, a thing that by its properties satisfies human wants of some sort or another. The nature of such wants, whether, for instance, they spring from the stomach or from fancy, makes no difference. . . .

The utility of a thing makes it a use-value. But this utility is not a thing of air. Being limited by the physical properties of the commodity, it has no existence apart from that commodity. A commodity, such as iron, corn, or a diamond, is therefore, so far as it is a material thing, a use-value, something useful. This property of a commodity is independent of the amount of labour required to appropriate its useful qualities. When treating of use-value, we always assume to be dealing with definite quantities, such as dozens of watches, yards of linen, or tons of iron. . . . Use values become a reality only by use or consumption: they also constitute the substance of all wealth, whatever may be the social form of that wealth. In the type of society we are about to consider [capitalist society], they are, in addition, the material depositories of exchange-value.

Exchange-value, at first sight, presents itself as a quantitative relation, as the proportion in which values in use of one sort are exchanged for those of another sort, a relation constantly changing with time and place. Here exchange-value appears to be something accidental and purely relative, and consequently, an intrinsic value. . . .

[T]he exchange-values of commodities must be capable of being expressed in terms of something common to them all, of which thing they represent a greater or less quantity.

This common "something" cannot be either a geometrical, a chemical, or any other natural property of commodities. Such properties claim our attention only in so far as they affect the utility of those commodities, make them use-values. But the exchange of commodities is evidently an act characterised by a total abstraction from use-value. Then one use-value is just as good as another. . . . As use-values, commodities are, above all, of different qualities, but as exchange-values they are merely different quantities, and consequently do not contain an atom of use-value.

## THINKING CRITICALLY

1. What is the use-value of a commodity? How is it determined?

2. What is the fundamental difference between a commodity's use-value and its exchange-value?

3. Do you think the real value of a commodity lies in its use-value or in its exchange-value? Explain.

# *Communist Manifesto*

In November 1847 the Communist League, a secretive international association of workers, met in London to draft a theoretical and practical program for their party. The *Communist Manifesto*, written by Karl Marx and Friedrich Engels, and excerpted here, has since become one of humankind's most controversial and studied political documents.

A spectre is haunting Europe—the spectre of Communism. All the Powers of old Europe have entered into a holy alliance to exorcise this spectre. . . .

Two things result from this fact.

I. Communism is already acknowledged by all European Powers to be itself a Power.

II. It is high time that Communists should openly, in the face of the whole world, publish their views, their aims, their tendencies, and meet this nursery tale of the spectre of Communism with a Manifesto [written statement] of the [Communist] party itself. . . .

The history of all hitherto existing society is the history of class struggles.

Freeman and slave, patrician and plebeian, lord and serf, guild-master and journeyman, in a word, oppressor and oppressed, stood in constant opposition to one another, carried on uninterrupted, now hidden, now open fight, a fight that each time ended, either in a revolutionary re-constitution of society at large, or in the common ruin of the contending [battling] classes. . . .

Society as a whole is more and more splitting up into two great hostile camps, into two great classes directly facing each other: Bourgeoisie and Proletariat. . . .

The bourgeoisie, wherever it has got the upper hand, has put an end to all feudal, patriarchal, idyllic relations. . . . It has resolved personal worth into exchange value, and in place of the numberless indefeasible [incapable of being undone] chartered freedoms, has set up that single, unconscionable [unprincipled] freedom—Free Trade. In one word, for exploitation, veiled by religious and political illusions, it has substituted naked, shameless, direct, brutal exploitation. . . .

In proportion as the bourgeoisie, *i.e.*, capital, is developed, in the same proportion is the proletariat, the modern working-class, developed, a class of laborers, who live only so long as they find work, and who find work only so long as their labor increases capital. These laborers, who must sell themselves piecemeal, are a commodity, like every other article of commerce, and are consequently exposed to all the vicissitudes [unpredictable changes] of competition, to all the fluctuations of the market. . . .

In what relation do the Communists stand to the proletarians as a whole? . . .

The distinguishing feature of Communism is not the abolition of property generally, but the abolition of bourgeois property. But modern bourgeois private property is the final and most complete expression of the system of producing and appropriating products, that is based on class antagonism, on the exploitation of the many by the few.

In this sense, the theory of the Communists may be summed up in the single sentence: Abolition of private property. . . .

You are horrified at our intending to do away with private property. But in your existing society private property is already done away with for nine-tenths of the population; its existence for the few is solely due to its non-existence in the hands of those nine-tenths. You reproach us, therefore, with intending to do away with a form of property, the necessary condition for whose existence is the non-existence of any property for the immense majority of society.

In one word, you reproach us with intending to do away with your property. Precisely so: that is just what we intend. . . .

The Communists are further reproached with desiring to abolish countries and nationalities.

The working men have no country. We cannot take from them what they don't possess. Since the proletariat must first of all acquire political supremacy, must rise to be the leading class of the nation, must constitute itself the nation, it is, so far, itself national, though not in the bourgeois sense of the word.

National differences and antagonisms between peoples are daily more and more vanishing, owing to the development of the bourgeoisie, to freedom of commerce, to the world-market, to uniformity in the mode of production and in the conditions of life corresponding thereto.

The supremacy of the proletariat will cause them to vanish still faster. United action, of the leading civilized countries at least, is one of the first conditions for the emancipation of the proletariat. . . .

The proletariat will use its political supremacy to wrest, by degrees, all capital from the bourgeoisie, to centralize all instruments of production in the hands of the State, *i.e.*, of the proletariat organized as a ruling class; and to increase the total productive forces as rapidly as possible.

Of course, in the beginning, this cannot be effected except by means of despotic inroads on the rights of property, and on the conditions of bourgeois production; by means of measures, therefore, which appear economically insufficient and untenable [unreasonable], but which in the course of the movement outstrip themselves, necessitate further inroads upon the old social order, and are unavoidable as a means of entirely revolutionizing the mode of production.

These measures will of course be different in different countries.

Nevertheless, in the most advanced countries the following will be pretty generally applicable:

1. Abolition of property in land and application of all rents of land to public purposes.
2. A heavy progressive or graduated income tax.
3. Abolition of all right of inheritance.
4. Confiscation of the property of all emigrants and rebels.
5. Centralization of credit in the hands of the State, by means of a national bank with State capital and an exclusive monopoly.
6. Centralization of the means of communication and transport in the hands of the State.
7. Extension of factories and instruments of production owned by the State; the bringing into cultivation of waste lands, and the improvement of the soil generally in accordance with a common plan.
8. Equal liability of all to labor. Establishment of industrial armies, especially for agriculture.
9. Combination of agriculture with manufacturing industries; gradual abolition of the distinction between town and country by a more equable distribution of the population over the country.
10. Free education for all children in public schools.

---

## THINKING CRITICALLY

1. According to Marx and Engels, what has the bourgeoisie sacrificed in pursuit of free trade?

2. According to Marx and Engels, what must happen before the proletariat will be free?

3. Although Marx and Engels envisioned communism as a system in which all people are equal, history has shown that communism carries many disadvantages for a people and a nation. What are these disadvantages?

# *Principles of Economics*

British economist Alfred Marshall was one of the leading figures in the development of modern economics. In the following excerpt from the *Principles of Economics*, originally published in 1890, Marshall explains the importance of economics as a social science and addresses the lack of interest in the study of economics among the world's great thinkers.

**P**olitical Economy or Economics is a study of mankind in the ordinary business of life; it examines that part of individual and social action which is most closely connected with the attainment and with the use of the material requisites [needs] of wellbeing.

Thus it is on the one side a study of wealth; and on the other, and more important side, a part of the study of man. For man's character has been moulded by his every-day work, and the material resources which he thereby procures [obtains], more than by any other influence unless it be that of his religious ideals. . . . Religious motives are more intense than economic, but their direct action seldom extends over so large a part of life. For the business by which a person earns his livelihood generally fills his thoughts during by far the greater part of those hours in which his mind is at its best; during them his character is being formed by the way in which he uses his faculties in his work, . . . and by his relations to his associates in work. . . .

And very often the influence exerted on a person's character by the amount of his income is hardly less, if it is less, than that exerted by the way in which it is earned. . . . [T]he conditions which surround extreme poverty, especially in densely crowded places, tend to deaden the higher faculties. . . . Overworked and undertaught, weary and careworn, without quiet and without leisure, they have no chance of making the best of their mental faculties. . . .

Broadly speaking, "the destruction of the poor is their poverty," and the study of the causes of poverty is the study of the causes of the degradation of a large part of mankind. . . .

It might have been expected that a science, which deals with questions so vital for the wellbeing of mankind, would have engaged the attention of many of the ablest thinkers of every age, and be now well advanced towards maturity. But the fact is that the number of scientific economists has always been small relatively to the difficulty of the work to be done. . . . One cause is of this is that the bearing of economics on the higher wellbeing of man has been overlooked. Indeed, a science which has wealth for its subject matter, is often repugnant at first sight to many students; for those who do most to advance the boundaries of knowledge, seldom care much about the possession of wealth for its own sake.

≈≈≈≈≈≈≈≈≈≈≈≈≈≈≈≈≈≈≈≈≈≈≈≈≈≈≈≈≈≈≈≈≈≈

## THINKING CRITICALLY

1. According to Marshall, why may economic motives have a greater impact on a person's actions than his or her religious beliefs?

2. To what does Marshall attribute the lack of attraction to the study of economics?

3. Do you agree that economic motives have such a great impact on people? Explain your answer.

# The Big Money

Henry Ford, one of the most influential industrialists in U.S. history, transformed the automobile industry and, in a sense, transformed the American way of life. In the following excerpt from *The Big Money*, novelist John Dos Passos uses an almost poetic style of writing to describe how Henry Ford's production methods and business practices brought about an era of social change.

For twenty years or more, ever since he'd left his father's farm when he was sixteen to get a job in a Detroit machineshop, Henry Ford had been nuts about machinery. First it was watches, then he designed a steamtractor, then he built a horseless carriage with an engine adapted from the Otto gasengine he'd read about in *The World of Science*, then a mechanical buggy with a one cylinder fourcycle motor, that would run forward but not back;

at last, in ninetyeight, he felt he was far enough along to risk throwing up his job with Detroit Edison Company, where he'd worked his way up from night fireman to chief engineer, to put all his time into working on a new gasoline engine,

(in the late eighties he'd met Edison at a meeting of electriclight employees in Atlantic City. He'd gone up to Edison after Edison had delivered an address and asked him if he thought gasoline was practical as a motor fuel. Edison had said yes. If Edison said it, it was true. Edison was the great admiration of Henry Ford's life);

and in driving his mechanical buggy, sitting there at the lever jauntily dressed in a tight-buttoned jacket and high collar and a derby hat, back and forth over the level illpaved streets of Detroit,

scaring the big brewery horses and the skinny trotting horses and the sleekrumped pacers with the motor's loud explosions,

looking for men scatterbrained enough to invest money in a factory for building automobiles.

He was the eldest son of an Irish immigrant who during the Civil War had married the daughter of a prosperous Pennsylvania Dutch farmer and settled down to farming near Dearborn in Wayne County, Michigan;

like plenty of other Americans, young Henry grew up hating the endless sogging through the mud about the chores, the hauling and pitching manure, the kerosene lamps to clean, the irk and sweat and solitude of the farm. . . .

He moved to Detroit, and in the brick barn behind his house tinkered for years in his spare time with a mechanical buggy that would be light enough to run over the clayey wagonroads of Wayne County, Michigan.

By 1900 he had a practicable [practical] car to promote. . . .

Henry Ford had ideas about other things than the designing of motors, carburetors, magnetos, jigs and fixtures, punches and dies; he had ideas about sales:

that the big money was in economical quantity production, quick turnover, cheap interchangeable easily replaced standardized parts:

it wasn't until 1909, after years of arguing with his partners, that Ford put out the first Model T.

Henry Ford was right.

That season he sold more than ten thousand tin lizzies, ten years later he was selling almost a million a year. . . .

In 1913 they established the assemblyline at Ford's. That season the profits were something like twentyfive million dollars, but they had trouble in keeping the men on the job, machinists didn't seem to like it at Ford's.

Henry Ford had ideas about other things than production.

He was the largest automobile manufacturer in the world; he paid high wages; maybe if the steady workers thought they were getting a cut (a very small cut) in the profits, it would give trained men an inducement [a reason] to stick to their jobs,

wellpaid workers might save enough money to buy a tin lizzie; the first day Ford's announcement that cleancut properlymarried American workers who wanted jobs had a chance to make five bucks a day (of course it turned out there were strings to it; always there were strings to it)

such an enormous crowd waited outside the Highland Park plant

all through the zero January night

that there was a riot when the gates were opened; cops broke heads, jobhunters threw bricks; property, Henry Ford's own property, was destroyed. The company dicks [armed guards] had to turn on the firehose to beat back the crowd.

The American Plan; automotive prosperity seeping down from above; it turned out there were strings to it.

But that five dollars a day

paid to good, clean American workmen

who didn't drink or smoke cigarettes or read or think, . . .

made all the tin lizzies and the automotive age, and incidentally,

made Henry Ford the automobileer, the admirer of Edison, the birdlover,

the great American of his time.

≈≈≈≈≈≈≈≈≈≈≈≈≈≈≈≈≈≈≈≈≈≈≈≈≈≈≈≈≈≈≈≈≈

## THINKING CRITICALLY

1. Where did Ford decide the "big money" was?
2. What problem did Ford run into after he started making a large profit? How did he remedy the situation?
3. How do you think Ford's policies would have to be altered in today's workplace?

# *Three Years Down*

The stock market boom of 1922 to 1929 brought unprecedented prosperity to all parts of the U.S. economy. Stock market investments were at an all-time high when, on Thursday, October 24, 1929, the stock market began to fall. The panic that followed led to the worst economic depression in the nation's history. In the following excerpt from his book *Three Years Down*, Jonathan Leonard recounts the details of the days between the initial fall and the final crash on "Black Tuesday."

That Saturday and Sunday Wall Street hummed with week-day activity. The great buildings were ablaze with lights all night as sleepy clerks fought desperately to get the accounts in shape for the Monday opening. Horrified brokers watched the selling orders accumulate. It wasn't a flood; it was a deluge. Everybody wanted to sell— the man with five shares and the man with ten thousand. . . .

Monday was a rout [retreat] for the banking pool, which was still supposed to be "on guard." If it did any net buying at all, which is doubtful, the market paid little attention. Leading stocks broke through the support levels as soon as trading started and kept sinking all day. . . .

When the market finally closed, 9,212,800 shares had been sold. The Times index of 25 industrials fell from 367.42 to 318.29. The whole list showed alarming losses. . . .

That night Wall Street was lit up like a Christmas tree. Restaurants, barber shops, and speakeasies were open and doing a roaring business. . . .

It wasn't only the financial bigwigs who spoke up. Even the outriders of the New Era felt that if everybody pretended to be happy, their phoney smiles would blow the trouble away. . . .

The next day, Tuesday, the 29th of October, was the worst of all. In the first half hour 3,259,800 shares were traded, almost a full day's work for the laboring machinery of the Exchange. The selling pressure was wholly without precedent. It was coming from everywhere. The wires to other cities were jammed with frantic orders to sell. So were the cables, radio and telephones to Europe and the rest of the world. Buyers were few, sometimes wholly absent. Often the specialists stood baffled at their posts, sellers pressing around them and not a single buyer at any price.

This was real panic. It was what the banks had prevented on Thursday, had slowed on Monday. Now they were helpless. . . .

When the closing bell rang, the great bull market was dead and buried. 16,410,000 shares had changed hands. Leading stocks had lost as much as 77% of their peak value. . . . Not only the little speculators, but the lordly, experienced big traders had been wiped out by the violence of the crash and the whole financial structure of the nation had been shaken to its foundations.

## THINKING CRITICALLY

1. What mistake did people make when stock values began to drop?
2. Why was Tuesday such a devastating day for the stock market?
3. What is the significance of Wall Street doing a roaring business on Monday night?

# "No Men Wanted"

The economic prosperity of the Roaring Twenties ended abruptly with the devastating stock market crash of 1929. In the following excerpt from the article "No Men Wanted," which originally appeared in the August 6, 1930, issue of *The Nation*, journalist Karl Monroe provides an account of how the Great Depression that followed the crash affected Americans from all walks of life.

With assets of perhaps twenty dollars and some nine years' experience as a reporter in New England I came to New York to find a job. The round of newspaper offices and news bureaus netted me a series of polite but firm statements to the effect that "there's nothing open just now, but you might leave your name and address." . . .

Innocently enough, I followed the crowd to the agencies in Sixth Avenue. Visions of being sent to a position where a percentage would be taken from the first month's salary for a fee were quickly dissolved in the face of the cold fact that any position must be paid for in full and in advance. I learned from one young man that he had paid $10 for a job at which he had worked only four days, receiving $13.50, or a net profit of $3.50 for his four days of work. He and other victims told me, apparently from experience, that many of the agencies make a regular practice of sending men to jobs for which they are obviously unfitted, so that the same job might be sold several times. Many of the men, I learned, realized this, but were willing to "take a gypping" in order to earn a few dollars. . . .

For three nights I slept in an institution on Twenty-third Street maintained for the benefit of released prisoners, who were given food and lodging until they found work. Along with others, I was given a hearty breakfast in the morning and a good meal at six at night, but none but jail-birds were aided in finding work. When I entered the place, on recommendation of a social-service agency, I had walked the streets for two days and nights, and my first real pleasure came when I found I could wash with hot water and soap. At the end of the three days the superintendent told me I must leave, explaining that the institution was maintained solely for ex-prisoners.

Finally, I stood in the bread line in Twenty-fifth Street. . . . To my surprise, I found in the line all types of men—the majority being skilled craftsmen unable to find work. One of them told me he had been a civil engineer and had earned $8,000 a year. Since losing his job almost a year ago, he had drifted from bad to worse, occasionally picking up odd jobs, until he had sunk to the bread line. . . .

There are many men who still hope despite months of failure. Of a dozen men in the park of nights, at least eight will tell you that they have something in mind for the following day, and they actually convince themselves. A few nights later a casual search will reveal the same men, still with "something in mind for tomorrow."

## THINKING CRITICALLY

1. Explain what was happening at the employment agencies.
2. Why was Monroe not offered more assistance at the institution?
3. Why do you think the economic hardships of the depression were as devastating emotionally as they were physically?

# *Price Making in a Democracy*

Many factors affect the price at which commodities and services are bought and sold. In the following excerpt from *Price Making in a Democracy*, first published in 1944, economist Edwin G. Nourse explains the balance between consumers' desire for low prices and the ability of retailers to offer them.

A long that frontier of the productive process where sellers of finished goods directly meet the ultimate consumer, we find one of the areas where low-price policies are most likely to flourish. This is a point at which the favorable results that price lowering may have on expansion of the business are promptly and clearly evident. . . . The great mass of consumers are poor by comparison with the abundance of their longings. The struggle to balance the budget of their wants makes them perennially "price conscious." To be sure, the ancient efforts of the individual buyer to "hammer down" prices through haggling at the store counter or in the market place have largely disappeared with the change in store methods and public manners. But even today the buyer of food and clothing and other personal items has many face-to-face opportunities to say to the merchant or the producer's representative, "Your price is too high; I'll go elsewhere," or perhaps, "I'll go without."

But the seller at retail may pursue a course of price lowering as a matter of voluntary policy, not as a mere yielding to duress [threat]. It is enlightening to think of the retail merchant as being in fact the purchasing agent for the housewife and for every other individual who seeks to command as many satisfactions as he can from his all-too-meager pay envelope or salary check. The merchant's professional attainment is to be measured by his ability to find cheaper sources of supply or to devise more economical means of assembling and distribution. . . .

Where distributors of finished goods grasp this concept of themselves as purchasing agents for the great body of consumers, they have extended a twofold influence in the direction of lower prices. First, they have sought to eliminate or reduce wastes and inefficiencies . . . in the process of assembling, handling, and passing on goods to the consumer. Second and more important, they have become in a sense professional representatives of the consumer, ranging farther than he possibly could in search of the most economical sources of supply, better equipped than he to discriminate differences in quality in relation to price and the uses to which an article is to be put, and aggressive in using the collective bargaining power of a large clientele to induce price concessions from the producer or to stir him to improvements in manufacturing methods or alterations in design which will make possible larger consumer satisfaction with less outlay.

≈≈≈≈≈≈≈≈≈≈≈≈≈≈≈≈≈≈≈≈≈≈≈≈≈≈≈≈≈≈≈≈≈≈≈≈

## THINKING CRITICALLY

1. Why are consumers so price conscious?
2. Why are retailers better able than consumers to lower prices?
3. According to Nourse's assertions, would it be more economical to shop at a local grocery market or at a chain supermarket? Why?

# *Why Alaska Needs Statehood*

The first bill for Alaskan statehood was introduced in Congress in 1916. However, the sustained campaign for statehood did not begin until the 1940s. In the following excerpt, then Governor Ernest Gruening makes an impassioned appeal for the extension of statehood to Alaska.

At the general election in October, 1946 the people of Alaska voted for statehood. . . .

The reasons for statehood are ample.

First: Alaskans, being good Americans and therefore believing that American citizenship is the most precious possession in the world, desire that citizenship in full measure. They do not have it now. They cannot vote for President or Vice President. They cannot elect Senators or a Representative with a vote. The Alaska legislature's powers are limited by obsolete restrictions imposed by Congress thirty-five years ago, many of which Alaskans have sought repeatedly and vainly to have changed.

Second: Statehood is indispensable [impossible to do without] for the progress and development of Alaska. . . .

An overshadowing problem is that of tuberculosis. Its incidence in Alaska is shocking—nine times that of the United States. . . . But the Congress has never appropriated adequately to meet this menace, which is becoming steadily aggravated by neglect. . . .

Similarly, the federal funds for education have been so cut that an increasing number of Indian and Eskimo children have been denied the basic American right to schooling, while hundreds of others have been turned over to the Territorial school system without the financial assistance to the Territory which Congress in similar situations invariably has furnished the States. . . .

Consider that Alaska is the only part of the American continent which stretches westward into the Eastern Hemisphere, and that its Pacific coast line is longer than that of our three Pacific states. . . . From the defense standpoint alone, the nation would be immeasurably strengthened by having in the halls of Congress two United States Senators and a Representative with a vote, intimately familiar with Alaska's vast terrain. . . .

But apart from that, Alaskans have another vital contribution to make. . . . The Alaskan is the robust type of individualist who is not afraid of hard work and is independent in thought and deed. Alaskans represent the vigorous survival of a spirit, an attitude, and a way of life that once was everywhere in America. They will contribute to the councils of the nation the initiative, the hardihood and the character which have built our great country. . . .

It is for Congress . . . to grant Alaska statehood NOW.

## THINKING CRITICALLY

1. What benefits was Gruening hoping to see for Alaska if statehood were granted?
2. What benefits did Gruening see Alaska providing for the United States?
3. Which of the arguments from the excerpt would you have found the most persuasive? Why?

# *Profiles in Courage*

Prior to being elected president, John F. Kennedy served as a U.S. senator from the state of Massachusetts. In the following excerpt from his 1955 Pulitzer Prize winning book *Profiles in Courage*, Kennedy discusses the many interests that a senator must balance.

The primary responsibility of a Senator, most people assume, is to represent the views of his state. Ours is a Federal system—a Union of relatively sovereign states whose needs differ greatly—and my Constitutional obligations as Senator would thus appear to require me to represent the interests of my state. Who will speak for Massachusetts if her own Senators do not? Her rights and even her identity become submerged. Her equal representation in Congress is lost. Her aspirations [goals], however much they may from time to time be in the minority, are denied that equal opportunity to be heard. . . .

Any Senator need not look very long to realize that his colleagues are representing *their* local interests. And if such interests are ever to be abandoned in favor of the national good, let the constituents—not the Senator—decide when and to what extent. . . .

But . . . we have not yet told the full story. For in Washington we are "United States Senators" and members of the Senate of the United States as well as Senators from Massachusetts and Texas. Our oath of office is administered by the Vice President, not by the Governors of our respective states; and we come to Washington . . . as members of the deliberative assembly [assembly whose role it is to make decisions] of one nation with one interest. Of course, we should not ignore the needs of our area—nor could we easily as products of that area—but none could be found to look out for the national interest if local interests wholly dominated the role of each of us.

There are other obligations in addition to those of state and region. . . . We believe in this country in the principle of party responsibility, and we recognize the importance of adhering to party platforms. . . .

But when party and officeholder differ as to how the national interest is to be served, we must place first the responsibility we owe not to our party or even to our constituents but to our individual consciences.

But it is a little easier to dismiss one's obligations to local interests and party ties than to face squarely the problem of one's responsibility to the will of his constituents. A Senator who avoids this responsibility would appear to be accountable to no one, and the basic safeguards of our democratic system would thus have vanished. . . .

In short, . . . if I am to be properly responsive to the will of my constituents, it is my duty to place their principles, not mine, above all else. This . . . is the essence of democracy, faith in the wisdom of the people and their views. To be sure, the people will make mistakes—they will get no better government than they deserve—but that is far better than the representative of the people arrogating [taking without authorization] for himself the right to say he knows better than they what is good for them. Is he not chosen, the argument closes, to vote as they would vote were they in his place?

## THINKING CRITICALLY

1. According to Kennedy, to what entities is a senator responsible?
2. In what situations should a senator go against local interests?
3. Why is a senator's primary responsibility to the constituents?

# *The Affluent Society*

In his book *The Affluent Society*, written in 1958 and revised several times, former Harvard economics professor John Kenneth Galbraith presented a critical look at the economic situation of the United States. The following excerpt highlights Galbraith's definition of the theory of consumer demand.

The theory of consumer demand, as it is now widely accepted, is based on two broad propositions, neither of them quite explicit but both extremely important for the present value system of economists. The first is that the urgency of wants does not diminish appreciably as more of them are satisfied or, to put the matter more precisely, to the extent that this happens, it is not demonstrable and not a matter of any interest to economists or for economic policy. When man has satisfied his physical needs, then psychologically grounded desires take over. These can never be satisfied or, in any case, no progress can be proved. The concept of satiation has very little standing in economics. It is held to be neither useful nor scientific to speculate on the comparative cravings of the stomach and the mind.

The second proposition is that wants originate in the personality of the consumer or, in any case, that they are given data for the economist. The latter's task is merely to seek their satisfaction. He has no need to inquire how these wants are formed. His function is sufficiently fulfilled by maximizing the goods that supply the wants. . . .

The notion that wants do not become less urgent the more amply the individual is supplied is broadly repugnant to common sense. It is something to be believed only by those who wish to believe. Yet the conventional wisdom must be tackled on its own terrain. Intertemporal comparisons of an individual's state of mind do rest on technically vulnerable ground. Who can say for sure that the deprivation which afflicts him with hunger is more painful than the deprivation which afflicts him with envy of his neighbor's new car? . . .

And emulation [imitation] has always played a considerable role in the views of other economists of want creation. One man's consumption becomes his neighbor's wish. This already means that the process by which wants are satisfied is also the process by which wants are created. The more wants that are satisfied, the more new ones are born. . . .

The even more direct link between production and wants is provided by the institutions of modern advertising and salesmanship. These cannot be reconciled with the notion of independently determined desires, for their central function is to create desires—to bring into being wants that previously did not exist. . . .

But such integration means recognizing that wants are dependent on production. It accords to the producer the function both of making the goods and of making the desires for them. It recognizes that production, not only passively through emulation, but actively through advertising and related activities, creates the wants it seeks to satisfy.

## THINKING CRITICALLY

1. Explain Galbraith's two assumptions about the theory of consumer demand.

2. How do producers create consumer demand?

3. Explain the relationship between emulation, wants, and consumer demand. Provide an example in which you have proven this theory to be true.

# *Silent Spring*

The publication in 1962 of Rachel Carson's book *Silent Spring*, a dark portrait of a world destroyed by the overuse of pesticides, helped spark an environmental movement that continues to this day. In the following excerpt from her book, Carson explains the consequences of the human desire to achieve "control of nature."

The history of life on earth has been a history of interaction between living things and their surroundings. To a large extent, the physical form and the habits of the earth's vegetation and its animal life have been molded by the environment. Considering the whole span of earthly time, the opposite effect, in which life actually modifies its surroundings, has been relatively slight. Only within the moment of time represented by the present century has one species—man—acquired significant power to alter the nature of his world.

During the past quarter century this power has not only increased to one of disturbing magnitude but it has changed in character. The most alarming of all man's assaults upon the environment is the contamination of air, earth, rivers, and sea with dangerous and even lethal materials. This pollution is for the most part irrecoverable [cannot be undone]; the chain of evil it initiates not only in the world that must support life but in living tissues is for the most part irreversible. In this now universal contamination of the environment, chemicals are the sinister and little-recognized partners of radiation in changing the very nature of the world—the very nature of its life. Strontium 90, released through nuclear explosions into the air, comes to earth in rain or drifts down as fallout, lodges in soil, enters into the grass or corn or wheat grown there, and in time takes up its abode in the bones of a human being, there to remain until his death. Similarly, chemicals sprayed on croplands or forests or gardens lie long in soil, entering into living organisms, passing from one to another in a chain of poisoning and death. Or they pass mysteriously by underground streams until they emerge and, through the alchemy of air and sunlight, combine into new forms that kill vegetation, sicken cattle, and work unknown harm on those who drink from once pure wells. As Albert Schweitzer has

said, "Man can hardly even recognize the devils of his own creation."

It took hundreds of millions of years to produce the life that now inhabits the earth—eons of time in which that developing and evolving and diversifying life reached a state of adjustment and balance with its surroundings. The environment, rigorously shaping and directing the life it supported, contained elements that were hostile as well as supporting. Certain rocks gave out dangerous radiation; even within the light of the sun, from which all life draws its energy, there were short-wave radiations with power to injure. Given time—time not in years but in millennia—life adjusts, and a balance has been reached. For time is the essential ingredient; but in the modern world there is no time.

The rapidity of change and the speed with which new situations are created follow the impetuous and heedless pace of . . . nature. Radiation is no longer merely the background radiation of rocks, the bombardment of cosmic rays, the ultraviolet of the sun that have existed before there was any life on earth; radiation is now the unnatural creation of man's tampering with the atom. The chemicals to which life is asked to make its adjustment are no longer merely the calcium and silica and copper and all the rest of the minerals washed out of the rocks and carried in rivers to the sea; they are the synthetic creations of man's inventive mind, brewed in his laboratories, and having no counterparts in nature.

To adjust to these chemicals would require time on the scale that is nature's; it would require not merely the years of a man's life but the life of generations. And even this, were it by some miracle possible, would be futile, for the new chemicals come from our laboratories in an endless stream; almost five hundred annually find their way into actual use in the United States alone. The figure is staggering and its implications are not easily grasped—500 new chemicals to which the bodies of men and animals are required somehow to adapt each year, chemicals totally outside the limits of biologic experience.

Among them are many that are used in man's war against nature. Since the mid-1940's over 200 basic chemicals have been created for use in killing insects, weeds, rodents, and other organisms described in the modern vernacular as "pests"; and they are sold under several thousand different brand names.

These sprays, dusts, and aerosols are now applied almost universally to farms, gardens, forests, and homes—nonselective chemicals that have the power to kill every insect, the "good" and the "bad," to still the song of birds and the leaping of fish in the streams, to coat the leaves with a deadly film, and to linger on in soil—all this though the intended target may be only a few weeds or insects. Can anyone believe it is possible to lay down such a barrage of poisons on the surface of the earth without making it unfit for all life? They should not be called "insecticides," but "biocides."

The whole process of spraying seems caught up in an endless spiral. Since DDT was released for civilian use, a process of escalation has been going on in which ever more toxic materials must be found. This has happened because insects, in a triumphant vindication of Darwin's principle of the survival of the fittest, have evolved super races immune to the particular insecticide used, hence a deadlier one has always to be developed—and then a deadlier one than that. . . .

The "control of nature" is a phrase conceived in arrogance, born of the Neanderthal age of biology and philosophy, when it was supposed that nature exists for the convenience of man. The concepts and practices of applied entomology [study of insects] for the most part date from that Stone Age of science. It is our alarming misfortune that so primitive a science has armed itself with the most modern and terrible weapons, and that in turning them against the insects it has also turned them against the earth.

≈≈≈≈≈≈≈≈≈≈≈≈≈≈≈≈≈≈≈≈≈≈≈≈≈≈≈≈≈≈≈≈≈≈≈≈

## THINKING CRITICALLY

1. Why is the contamination of the air, earth, and water the most evil of human assaults?

2. What are the dangers of insecticides?

3. What does Carson mean by the phrase "control of nature?" How can efforts to control nature be harmful?

# Abe Fortas's Opinion in re Gault

In 1964 Gerald Gault, a 15-year-old boy, was arrested and charged with making an obscene telephone call to a neighbor. In re Gault ("In the Matter of Gault") was the first case involving a juvenile to reach the U.S. Supreme Court. The landmark case extended the constitutional rights of due process of law to juveniles. The majority opinion in the case, written by Justice Abe Fortas in 1967, is excerpted here.

From the inception [beginning] of the juvenile court system, wide differences have been tolerated—indeed insisted upon—between the procedural rights accorded to adults and those of juveniles. In practically all jurisdictions, there are rights granted to adults which are withheld from juveniles. In addition to the specific problems involved in the present case, for example, it has been held that the juvenile is not entitled to bail, to indictment by grand jury, to a public trial or to trial by jury. It is frequent practice that rules governing the arrest and interrogation [questioning] of adults by the police are not observed in the case of juveniles.

Failure to observe the fundamental requirements of due process has resulted in instances, which might have been avoided, of unfairness to individuals and inadequate or inaccurate findings of fact and unfortunate prescriptions of remedy. Due process of law is the primary and indispensable foundation of individual freedom. . . .

[I]t would be extraordinary if our Constitution did not require the procedural regularity and the exercise of care implied in the phrase "due process." Under our Constitution, the condition of being a boy does not justify a kangaroo court [mock court in which the principles of law and justice are disregarded]. . . .

We conclude that the Due Process Clause of the Fourteenth Amendment requires that in respect of proceedings to determine delinquency which may result in commitment to an institution in which the juvenile's freedom is curtailed, the child and his parents must be notified of the child's right to be represented by counsel retained by them, or . . . appointed to represent the child.

We conclude that the constitutional privilege against self-incrimination is applicable in the case of juveniles as it is with respect to adults. . . . We appreciate that special problems may arise with respect to waiver of the privilege by or on behalf of children, and that there may well be some difference in technique—but not in principle—depending upon the age of the child and the presence and competence of parents.

≈≈≈≈≈≈≈≈≈≈≈≈≈≈≈≈≈≈≈≈≈≈≈≈≈≈≈≈≈≈≈≈≈

## THINKING CRITICALLY

1. What fundamental rights was Gault denied?
2. Who must be notified of an accused juvenile's rights?
3. According to Justice Fortas, what is the foundation of an individual's freedom? Do you agree or disagree? Explain.

# A Theory of Justice

John Rawls, a professor of philosophy at Harvard University, is considered one of the most noted political philosophers of the twentieth century. His 1971 work *A Theory of Justice*, from which the introduction is excerpted here, is regarded as a modern version of Rousseau's *Social Contract*.

Justice is the first virtue of social institutions, as truth is of systems of thought. A theory however elegant and economical must be rejected or revised if it is untrue; likewise laws and institutions no matter how efficient and well-arranged must be reformed or abolished if they are unjust. Each person possesses an inviolability [sanctity] founded on justice that even the welfare of society as a whole cannot override. For this reason justice denies that the loss of freedom for some is made right by a greater good shared by others. It does not allow that the sacrifices imposed on a few are outweighed by the larger sum of advantages enjoyed by many. Therefore in a just society the liberties of equal citizenship are taken as settled; the rights secured by justice are not subject to political bargaining or to the calculus of social interests. The only thing that permits us to acquiesce [comply] in an erroneous theory is the lack of a better one; analogously, an injustice is tolerable only when it is necessary to avoid an even greater injustice. Being first virtues of human activities, truth and justice are uncompromising. . . .

Let us assume, to fix ideas, that a society is a more or less self-sufficient association of persons who in their relations to one another recognize certain rules of conduct as binding and who for the most part act in accordance with them. Suppose further that these rules specify a system of cooperation designed to advance the good of those taking part in it. Then, although a society is a cooperative venture for mutual advantage, it is typically marked by a conflict as well as by an identity of interests. . . . These principles are the principles of social justice: they provide a way of assigning rights and duties in the basic institutions of society and they define the appropriate distribution of the benefits and burdens of social cooperation. . . .

Existing societies are of course seldom well-ordered in this sense, for what is just and unjust is usually in dispute. Men disagree about which principles should define the basic terms of their association. Yet we may still say, despite this disagreement, that they each have a concept of justice. . . . Those who hold different conceptions of justice can, then, still agree that institutions are just when no arbitrary distinctions are made between persons in the assigning of basic rights and duties and when the rules determine a proper balance between competing claims to the advantages of social life.

## THINKING CRITICALLY

1. According to Rawls, is injustice ever tolerable? If so, when?
2. What are the purposes of the principles of justice?
3. How would the existence of discrimination in a society affect Rawls's theory of social justice?

# The Evolution of International Economic Order

Former Princeton professor W. Arthur Lewis was a leader in the study of developmental economics. In the following excerpt from *The Evolution of International Economic Order*, published in 1978, Lewis describes the factors that divided the world into industrialized and agricultural countries.

How did the world come to be divided into industrial countries and agricultural countries? . . .

At the end of the eighteenth century, trade between what are now the industrial countries and what is now the Third World was based on geography rather than on structure. . . .

In the course of the first half of the nineteenth century industrialization changed the composition of the trade, since Britain captured world trade in iron and in cotton fabrics; but the volume of trade with the Third World continued to be small. . . .

There are two reasons for this low volume of trade. One is that the leading industrial countries—Britain, the United States, France, and Germany—were, taken together, virtually self-sufficient. The raw materials of the industrial revolution were coal, iron ore, cotton, and wool, and the foodstuff was wheat. Between them, these core countries had all they needed except for wool. . . .

The second reason why trade was so small is that the expansion of world trade, which created the international economic order that we are considering, is necessarily an offshoot of the transport revo-

lutions. In this case, the railway was the major element. Before the railway the external trade of Africa or Asia or Latin America was virtually though not completely confined to the seacoasts and rivers; the railway altered this. Although the industrial countries were building railways from 1830 on, the railway did not reach the Third World until the 1860s. . . .

[T]he world began to divide into industrial and nonindustrial countries.

Why did it happen this way? . . .

We must . . . turn to economic explanations. The most important of these, and the most neglected, is the dependence of an industrial revolution on a prior or simultaneous agricultural revolution. . . .

In a closed economy, the size of the industrial sector is a function of agricultural productivity. Agriculture has to be capable of producing the surplus food and raw materials consumed in the industrial sector. . . . If the domestic market is too small, it is still possible to support an industrial sector by exporting manufactures and importing food and raw materials. But it is hard to begin industrialization by exporting manufactures.

≈≈≈≈≈≈≈≈≈≈≈≈≈≈≈≈≈≈≈≈≈≈≈≈≈≈≈≈≈≈≈≈≈≈

## THINKING CRITICALLY

1. Why was the trade volume between industrial and agricultural countries low in the 1800s?

2. According to Lewis, why is an industrial revolution dependent on a prior agricultural revolution?

3. What long-term problems do you think can result from a lack of industrialization and development?

# "Congress: The First Two Hundred Years"

Today, more than 200 years after the drafting of the U.S. Constitution, the structure of the federal government it created remains relatively unchanged. Still, Congress has changed in a number of ways. In the following excerpt from the article "Congress: The First Two Hundred Years," first published in *National Forum* in 1984, then Speaker of the House Thomas P. "Tip" O'Neill, Jr., describes the growth and development of political parties in the United States and their effect on the workings of Congress.

As we approach the Bicentennial of the Constitution and the Congress it created, it is appropriate to consider how the legislative branch of our federal government has developed during its nearly 200 years of existence. . . .

Take the development of political parties, for example. It is hard to imagine our government functioning without a strong two-party system. Yet the Continental Congress and the Articles of Confederation Congress existed without parties. The idea of political parties apparently never arose at the Constitutional Convention, either. . . .

We normally consider the role of political parties in the House or the Senate only in terms of partisan votes on legislative issues or the means for selection of internal leadership positions. The existence of political parties, however, has changed dramatically the basic relationship between the Congress and the president in a way unanticipated in 1787.

Specifically, when the Constitutional Convention considered the method of electing the president, only one state delegation—Pennsylvania—felt that the president of the United States should be elected directly by the people. After much discussion and negotiation, the delegates decided upon indirect election of the president, using electors meeting in their separate states to cast their votes. Because of the lack of communications facilities at the time and the lack of nationally popular leaders other than George Washington, it was commonly assumed that the electoral vote generally would be indecisive. . . .

How, then, did the delegates think that the president would be elected? The answer, found in Article II, Section 1 of the Constitution, is that the House of Representatives—each state delegation having one vote—would usually elect the president. The candidate with the majority of state delegations would become president. The second-place finisher would become vice president. If there were a tie for second, the Senate would choose the vice presidency. Coupled with modifications by the Twelfth Amendment to the Constitution, this is the arrangement today.

The two-party system completely wrecked this carefully wrought plan, for only twice (Thomas Jefferson in 1801 and John Quincy Adams in 1825) has the House been called upon to elect the president. This is not to say that the way things have developed is bad or wrong. On the contrary, I believe we have a much better system than anticipated. But the plan to make the president dependent upon the Congress for election in most instances was all part of the balance designed by the men who wrote the Constitution. . . .

Even during my thirty-some years in Congress, the party system has changed a lot, and some of these changes have hurt the ability of Congress to act effectively. When I first entered the House in 1953, it seemed that most of the members had worked their way up through the ranks to get to the House of Representatives. They had worked for their party on the local or state level and had served in some kind of local office . . . and they knew what it meant to follow the leadership and learn the art of legislation. There were not many members in those days who set out on their own with complete disregard for the party to which they belonged.

They had some understanding of government and how it works.

The party system is much different today, and I believe it works to our detriment as a Congress. Men and women are elected to the House without having previously held elective office. They can get elected because they raise the money and hire a media consultant and get on television. Some of them do not care about what party they belong to, and they feel as if they owe the party nothing when they take office. . . . The result has been a breakdown of party discipline and a refusal to follow party leadership, which leads in turn to congressional paralysis and an inability to act coherently as a legislative body.

## THINKING CRITICALLY

1. How did the framers of the Constitution envision that the president would be elected?

2. According to O'Neill, how did the party system change during his some 30 years in Congress?

3. Does O'Neill believe that recent changes in political parties have helped or hurt U.S. government? Do you agree?

# *Contract with America*

On September 27, 1994, in a ceremony held on the steps of the U.S. Capitol, more than 300 Republican candidates for the House of Representatives signed a document called the *Contract with America*. The contract, developed by Representative Newt Gingrich, who was next in line to become Speaker of the House, was a pledge to voters that, if elected, the representatives would pass specific bills designed to reform congressional procedures. The contract had its desired effect, for in the November elections the Republicans won control of both houses of Congress for the first time in two generations.

As Republican Members of the House of Representatives and as citizens seeking to join that body we propose not just to change its policies, but even more important, to restore the bonds of trust between the people and their elected representatives.

That is why, in this era of official evasion and posturing, we offer instead a detailed agenda for national renewal, a written commitment with no fine print.

This year's election offers the chance, after four decades of one-party control, to bring to the House a new majority that will transform the way Congress works. That historic change would be the end of government that is too big, too intrusive, and too easy with the public's money. It can be the beginning of a Congress that respects the values and shares the faith of the American family.

Like Lincoln, our first Republican president, we intend to act "with firmness in the right, as God gives us to see the right." To restore accountability to Congress. To end its cycle of scandal and disgrace. To make us all proud again of the way free people govern themselves.

On the first day of the 104th Congress, the new Republican majority will immediately pass the following major reforms, aimed at restoring the faith and trust of the American people in their government:

**FIRST**, require all laws that apply to the rest of the country also apply equally to the Congress;

**SECOND**, select a major, independent auditing firm to conduct a comprehensive audit of Congress for waste, fraud or abuse;

**THIRD**, cut the number of House committees, and cut committee staff by one-third;

**FOURTH**, limit the terms of all committee chairs;

**FIFTH**, ban the casting of proxy votes in committee;

**SIXTH**, require committee meetings to be open to the public;

**SEVENTH**, require a three-fifths majority vote to pass a tax increase;

**EIGHTH**, guarantee an honest accounting of our Federal Budget by implementing zero baseline budgeting.

Thereafter, within the first 100 days of the 104th Congress, we shall bring to the House Floor the following bills, each to be given full and open debate, each to be given a clear and fair vote and each to be immediately available this day for public inspection and scrutiny.

### 1. The Fiscal Responsibility Act

A balanced budget/tax limitation amendment and a legislative line-item veto to restore fiscal responsibility to an out-of-control Congress, requiring them to live under the same budget constraints as families and businesses.

### 2. The Taking Back Our Streets Act

An anti-crime package including stronger truth-in-sentencing, "good faith" exclusionary rule exemptions, effective death penalty provisions, and cuts in social spending from this summer's "crime" bill to fund prison construction and additional law enforcement to keep people secure in their neighborhoods and kids safe in their schools.

### 3. The Personal Responsibility Act

Discourage illegitimacy and teen pregnancy by prohibiting welfare to minor mothers and denying increased AFDC for additional children while on welfare, cut spending for welfare programs, and enact a tough two-years-and-out provision with work requirements to promote individual responsibility.

### 4. The Family Reinforcement Act

Child support enforcement, tax incentives for adoption, strengthening rights of parents in their children's education, stronger child pornography laws, and an elderly dependent care tax credit to reinforce the central role of families in American society.

### 5. The American Dream Restoration Act

A $500 per child tax credit, begin repeal of the marriage tax penalty, and creation of American Dream Savings Accounts to provide middle class tax relief.

### 6. The National Security Restoration Act

No U.S. troops under U.N. command and restoration of the essential parts of our national security funding to strengthen our national defense and maintain our credibility around the world.

### 7. The Senior Citizens Fairness Act

Raise the Social Security earnings limit which currently forces seniors out of the work force, repeal the 1993 tax hikes on Social Security benefits and provide tax incentives for private long-term care insurance to let Older Americans keep more of what they have earned over the years.

### 8. The Job Creation and Wage Enhancement Act

Small business incentives, capital gains cut and indexation, neutral cost recovery, risk assessment/cost-benefit analysis, strengthening the Regulatory Flexibility Act and unfunded mandate reform to create jobs and raise worker wages.

### 9. The Common Sense Legal Reform Act

"Loser pays" laws, reasonable limits on punitive damages and reform of product liability laws to stem the endless tide of litigation [lawsuits].

### 10. The Citizen Legislature Act

A first-ever vote on term limits to replace career politicians with citizen legislators.

Further, we will instruct the House Budget Committee to report to the floor and we will work to enact additional budget savings, beyond the budget cuts specifically included in the legislation described above, to ensure that the Federal budget deficit will be less than it would have been without the enactment of these bills.

Respecting the judgment of our fellow citizens as we seek their mandate for reform, we hereby pledge our names to this Contract with America.

---

## THINKING CRITICALLY

1. Briefly describe the reforms in congressional procedures specified in the contract.

2. What reforms does the contract propose in support of families?

3. Do you think this type of document is a useful means of understanding a party's platform, or do you think it was political propaganda used to win votes? Explain.

## READING 1

1. Similar elements include that an individual's rights cannot be infringed upon without lawful proceedings, that people accused of crimes are entitled to be judged by their peers, and that accused people have the right to a speedy trial.
2. The government could infringe upon a person's freedom of movement in times of war or when it was deemed necessary for the common good of the kingdom.
3. Answers will vary slightly. Examples include: trial by jury, representation for taxation, no one—not even a king—is above the law, freedom of movement, and freedom from religious persecution.

## READING 2

1. They made the voyage to establish a colony in the northern parts of Virginia.
2. They signed the Compact to preserve and order the new colony.
3. Answers will vary but should demonstrate an understanding of the necessity of laws and social cooperation.

## READING 3

1. Parliament is complaining that despite previous laws disallowing unlegislated taxation, people still have been forced to lend money to the king and have been taxed without the consent of Parliament.
2. Parliament is protesting the practice of martial law.
3. The right of petition allows citizens to ask their government to do or not do certain things. It is important because it allows citizens to make their wishes known to their government.

## READING 4

1. The government was to have one governor, one deputy governor, and eighteen assistants.
2. According to the charter, new government officials were to come to office by being elected and chosen out of the freemen of the Company.
3. Answers will vary. Students may say that having the charter in the colony freed the colonists from having to rely on the government in England to interpret the provisions of the charter, and that the great distance between the colony and England made the colonists less willing to seek the approval of the English government when making any changes.

## READING 5

1. The commonwealth was established to maintain the peace and union of the people.

2. The Fundamental Orders states that when money must be levied it must be done by the common consent of the General Court and that a committee must be chosen to set the amount of taxes. The committee must represent all towns equally.
3. The Mayflower Compact is a general agreement to establish a form of self-government. Unlike the Fundamental Orders, however, the Mayflower Compact does not set up a detailed organization of government. The Fundamental Orders is considered by some to be the first constitution in the colonies because of its detailed plan of government.

## READING 6

1. King James attempted to eliminate the Protestant religion and disregarded the laws and liberties of the kingdom.
2. Citizens are guaranteed the right to vote, to petition the king, and to participate on juries.
3. The Bill of Rights makes references to the powers of the king, thus the English government is a system in which Parliament and the king share power.

## READING 7

1. The stated purpose is to join in a bond of friendship to support the common defense and to secure the liberties and general welfare of the states.
2. Each state legislature was to determine how its delegates would be chosen.
3. The Articles stated that no person in any state or in Congress shall grant or be granted a title of nobility.
4. A state could engage in war without the consent of Congress only if it were invaded by enemies or had received word that the Indians were planning to invade.
5. The government was to be financed by taxation monitored by the state legislatures.
6. Article IX denies the ability of the nation to deny a state any of its territory.
7. Congress has the power to establish and monitor the postal system.
8. Congress must receive the votes of nine states to exercise most of its powers.
9. Article IX states that Congress must publish its journal monthly and that the states may at any time request a copy of the journal.
10. Canada was offered the opportunity to join the confederation.
11. The new confederacy honored all debts acquired by the states prior to the formation of the confederation.

12. Answers will vary but students should understand the drawbacks to having a nation governed by a weak central government.

## READING 8

1. The stated purposes are to remind people of their rights and duties, to ensure that the acts of the legislature and the executive are in accordance with the desires of the governed, and to ensure that the demands of the citizens will always be guided toward the preservation of the constitution.
2. The declaration states that a common contribution is necessary for the maintenance of public institutions, but that the cost should be equitably distributed according to people's means; that people have the right to know how the funds are being used; and that the mode of assessment, means of collection, and duration of taxation should be uniform.
3. According to the declaration, the purpose of government is to preserve the natural rights of people. This is similar to the Declaration of Independence in that it also states that governments are instituted among people to preserve people's inalienable rights.

## READING 9

1. The flag signifies the nation that Americans were fighting to preserve. "The land of the free" should be interpreted as a reference to freedom from British rule. Students could also interpret it as a statement about the democratic nature of the U.S. government.
2. Key is referring to the British.
3. Answers will vary but students should understand the historical significance of "The Star-Spangled Banner" as the national anthem.

## READING 10

1. The United States would make preparations for defense only when the nation's rights are invaded or seriously threatened.
2. Any intrusion on any free and independent nation would be viewed as a direct threat to the United States.
3. Monroe is adhering to a policy of isolationism. He advanced this policy by stating that the United States would not interfere in any European affairs and would only make defense preparations if the United States or another free nation was threatened.

## READING 11

1. They state that men have deprived women of their right to vote, subjected women to laws that they did not help create, stripped women of their right to own property or receive an education, and basically denied women all the civil and legal rights accorded to men.
2. The resolutions state that women must be viewed as the equal of men, and as such, be afforded the same rights and responsibilities extended to men. They also state that it is a woman's duty to secure her own freedoms.
3. Answers will vary. Examples include an understanding of the relationship between the fight for independence of a nation and the fight for independence of a specific group within the population of that nation; or the irony that a nation founded on the principles of liberty and equality denies these fundamental rights to half its population.

## READING 12

1. The Emancipation Proclamation applied to people held as slaves in states or any portions of states that were in rebellion against the U.S. government.
2. Lincoln stated that Congress would be held on January 1 and that any state whose legally and democratically elected members attended the session would be deemed not in rebellion.
3. The Emancipation Proclamation transformed the war from primarily an effort to preserve the Union into a crusade to end slavery. It also ensured that European powers would not intervene on the side of the Confederacy.

## READING 13

1. The United States is asking Germany to agree to—and help persuade other countries to agree to—the following: not interfere with trade occurring in any Chinese ports; allow China to collect duties; and not discriminate, for the purpose of levying tariffs, on the basis of national origin.
2. Hay was confident that Great Britain and Japan would agree to the terms of the policy because their commercial interests were at stake.
3. Students may answer that it was wise to adopt an open-door policy with China because China has the fastest growing economy in the world. Students may answer no, but should provide a logical explanation for their answer.

## READING 14

1. The goals are freedom to vote, equal opportunity for education, open trials, responsibility of sitting on juries, defense against lynching, equal service on all carriers, equal rights to use public facilities for which they pay equal taxes, equal opportunity for

employment, replacement of the phrase "black American" with "American."

2. It is also the white person's fight because equality of all citizens is the fundamental basis of democracy. By extending equal rights to all U.S. citizens, the United States could achieve in reality the type of democracy it practices in theory.

3. Social equality is a matter of personal choice. All people are free to believe as they choose. Public equality, however, occurs when the government abandons the prejudices of individuals and treats all people, regardless of race, as equals. Answers should also include a statement of opinion concerning the causal relationship between public equality and social equality.

### READING 15

1. One of the primary objectives is to create conditions in which nations will be able to establish a way of life that is not subject to coercion.

2. Truman believes that assistance should be given through economic aid and civilian and military assistance in the tasks of reconstruction. This will allow nations to secure their own economic stability and orderly political processes.

3. Although the document does not explicitly use the word communism, the Truman Doctrine was the first foreign-policy agenda aimed solely at stopping the advances of Communist forces. It launched the foreign-policy agenda of containment, a policy that the United States would follow for the next 40 years. Answers should also include an assessment of the wisdom of the policy of containment.

### READING 16

1. The purpose is to establish a common standard of human rights to which all people and all nations will be held.

2. Both documents call for fundamental freedoms such as speech, assembly, and religion; both detail a person's rights of due process and security from cruel punishment; both guarantee freedom from imposition in the home. The U.S. Bill of Rights does not specifically mention the word "privacy" and does not address marriage. The Universal Declaration does not address the right to bear arms.

3. The declaration supports a democratic form of government, as described in Article 21.

### READING 17

1. The president-elect is promising to defend the freedoms and institutions of the United States.

2. The president-elect makes the promise to the people of the United States.

3. The founders wanted to ensure that the president would abide by the provisions of the Constitution and would be responsible to the people of the United States.

### READING 18

1. All three documents profess an allegiance to the United States and to the liberties that the nation ensures.

2. Both the pledge and the creed mention the indivisibility of the nation, and the oath of citizenship states that, as citizens, people must defend the country against all enemies, foreign and domestic.

3. Answers will vary but students should remark on the importance and impact of pledges, creeds, and oaths.

### READING 19

1. Henry distrusts the British government because even as the British graciously accepted American petitions, they were making preparations for war.

2. Henry is asking the people to fight the British in defense of American independence.

3. Henry is appealing to the people's desire for freedom. He states that Britain is never going to grant America its independence and thus, to secure their own sovereignty, war is inevitable. Answers should also include several lines quoted from the speech that students believe are the most convincing.

### READING 20

1. Henry believes that the government will be consolidated and that the interests of the people will be addressed only in their relation to the nation as a whole.

2. Madison states that it will create a consolidated government because it will address the people as a whole, but also that it will be federal in nature because it will address the people of the 13 states.

3. Answers will vary but should present an opinion of whether people generally view the United States as predominantly concerned with preserving national interests or as a nation built on the fundamental interests of each of the states.

### READING 21

1. Washington believes it is dangerous to form such attachments because they provide a false sense of common interests.

2. Washington states that parties are the true enemy of popular forms of government because they distract

the public council from governing, create unfounded suspicions, promote animosity, and leave an opportunity for the interference of foreign governments.

3. Washington is advocating a policy of isolationism. Students should provide examples from the excerpt that point to this policy.

## READING 22

1. Jefferson says that the will of the majority must prevail but that it must be rightful and also protect the rights of the minority.

2. Jefferson is asking the people to practice political tolerance.

3. Answers will vary. Students who say it is possible for opposing parties to work together may point out that the good of the nation should override political differences. Students who say it is not possible may point to constant opposition between the Republican Congress and the president during the Clinton administration.

## READING 23

1. The people dedicating the cemetery cannot consecrate the field because the men who had fought there to preserve their country had already consecrated it.

2. Lincoln says that the people must increase their devotion to the cause for which the soldiers lost their lives.

3. Answers will vary but students should understand that the central purpose of President Lincoln's speech was to regenerate support and dedication to the cause of preserving the Union.

## READING 24

1. U.S. government is based on the theory of equality for all people.

2. She states that men's right to vote is not necessarily secure because state constitutions could at any time make provisions to deny the right to vote to a specific sector of the male population; thus the proposed amendment will guarantee that the right to vote will be extended to all citizens and denied only for reasons applicable to all citizens.

3. Anthony explains that the U.S. government was based on perfect equality for all citizens, but by denying women the right to vote it was denying equal rights to half the nation's population.

## READING 25

1. The holders of fixed investment favored the gold standard and the common masses favored the silver standard.

2. Bryan says that their definition of a businessman is too narrow and that the working masses are as much businessmen as their employers.

3. One of the central arguments against the silver standard was that other nations did not use it. By addressing U.S. independence from Britain, Bryan was appealing to the emotions of a nation founded on a recent struggle for sovereignty.

## READING 26

1. Roosevelt's main complaint against corporations is the political influence they wield.

2. Roosevelt is calling for increased governmental control of business.

3. Roosevelt states that a full reporting of business practices needs to be made public; thus it is the individual's responsibility to research a company with whom he or she is planning to conduct business. Students should also state whether or not they think this will be effective, for example, whether or not people are conscientious enough to seek out the information.

## READING 27

1. According to Wilson, a trust is arranged to get rid of competition, and a big business survives because of competition.

2. Trusts harm the consumer because they stifle competition and thus the consumer is forced to pay higher prices. Also, when a trust buys out a small business and incurs a loss of profit, the consumer must pay the interest on the loss.

3. Freedom of opportunity is central to U.S. democracy and by stifling competition, freedom of opportunity is also stifled.

## READING 28

1. The readjustment of all colonial claims relates to the notion of securing free political and economic opportunity for the people of the world.

2. He was calling for the creation of the League of Nations.

3. The United States must be partners in the process of peace because the world itself must be fit to live in and until justice is done to others, it will not be done to the United States. Answers should also include an assessment of Wilson's reasoning.

## READING 29

1. Mr. Harrison points out to the assembly that no senator can speak on the same topic more than twice in the same day.

2. Mr. Long would have yielded the floor had he asked for an official roll call. He asked for the inquiry so that he could continue stalling.
3. Filibusters block the will of the majority, which is the basis of democratic government; they are costly to U.S. taxpayers because Senate is in session and nothing is being accomplished; and they waste time when other legislation could be discussed.

## READING 30
1. Americans expect from their government equality of opportunity, jobs for those who can work, security, civil liberties, scientific progress, and a rising standard of living.
2. Students should describe freedom of speech and expression, freedom of religion, secure economic standing, and the reduction of armaments. Roosevelt wanted each of these freedoms to be guaranteed to people throughout the world.
3. Roosevelt claimed that the United States was fighting for the preservation of democratic life in the United States and for a new world order of cooperation between free governments everywhere.

## READING 31
1. Kennedy says that the only way to ensure that the arms will not be used is if there are enough of them produced to ensure both sides of complete destruction. Students should also state whether they agree or disagree with this point of view.
2. Kennedy is asking the American people to be prepared to defend and serve their country if the need should arise.
3. The main focus of the speech is the possibility of the need for defensive action. Students will probably say that this type of speech would not be appropriate today because, in today's society, issues such as the economy, crime, and AIDS are more pressing than the threat of war.

## READING 32
1. King asks that they continue the struggle through nonviolent action.
2. King's dream is that the nation will eventually live up to the ideal that all people are created equal, and that people will cease to be judged by the color of their skin.
3. The significance is that Abraham Lincoln, the man who delivered the Emancipation Proclamation, had begun a reform movement 100 years prior and yet African Americans still did not enjoy the equal rights that accompany U.S. citizenship.

## READING 33
1. Chávez fasted in order to call nationwide attention to the plight of farmworkers.
2. He says that participation and self-determination remain the best experience of freedom. Students should also explain why they agree or disagree with this statement.
3. Mohandas Gandhi was a strong advocate of nonviolent protest during the movement for independence in India. Martin Luther King, Jr., was also a supporter of nonviolent protest.

## READING 34
1. According to Agnew, the television news medium has the fewest checks on its power.
2. Newspeople decide how issues are presented and interpreted, Americans know very little about the newspeople who make these decisions, and the newspeople do not reflect the views of the majority of Americans.
3. Answers will vary but should include a logical reflection on the validity of Agnew's remarks, as well as provide examples when the television news medium has had an overwhelming influence on public opinion.

## READING 35
1. He addresses the environmental impact of population growth and the threat to the world's supply of fresh water.
2. He states that developed countries have a disproportionate impact on the environment. These countries have less than a quarter of the world's population and yet they use three quarters of the world's resources.
3. The purpose of this speech is to make people understand the imminent dangers that are threatening the global environment. Students should also comment on their feelings about this speech.

## READING 36
1. Jefferson states that forcing a person to furnish money in support of opinions in which he or she does not believe is sinful and tyrannical.
2. Jefferson argues that religious opinion should no more be a factor in determining a person's civil rights than his or her opinion about physics or geometry.
3. According to Jefferson, the natural weapons of humans are free argument and debate. Armed with these weapons, humans will naturally come to the truth; without them, errors will prevail because no one would have the power to contradict them.

## READING 37

1. The 13 districts are divided into three circuits. Each circuit has two courts called circuit courts, each of which consists of two Supreme Court justices and the district court from the district of which the circuit court is a part. Circuit court's jurisdiction includes: civil cases exceeding $500 to which the United States or an alien is a party, or the suit is between citizens of different states. It also has appellate jurisdiction in all cases from the district courts.
2. The Supreme Court has original jurisdiction over most civil cases to which states are a party, and over suits involving ambassadors or public officials; and appellate jurisdiction over all cases from the circuit courts and state courts.
3. The decision was based on Article VI of the Constitution, which states that the U.S. Constitution has supremacy over state laws.

## READING 38

1. The stated purpose was to extend the protection of U.S. laws to Native Americans.
2. An Indian would be eligible for citizenship if he or she was born in the United States, complied with the provisions of the Dawes Act, and adopted the habits of "civilized life."
3. Some Native Americans resisted the act because they chose to continue their tribal traditions.

## READING 39

1. The act states that no person, corporation, or association shall be granted undue preference, and that no carrier shall charge greater or lesser fares to anyone for comparable services.
2. Section 5 addresses the formation of monopolies.
3. Students who believe that government interferes too much in business may say that such overregulation impedes on the freedom of business to seek profit. Students who disagree with this view may say that regulation is needed to protect the interests of consumers.

## READING 40

1. This act applies to all persons, corporations, and associations conducting business within the United States or with foreign nations.
2. Original jurisdiction rests in the circuit courts of the United States.
3. The act would be difficult to enforce because many key terms, such as "trust" and "restraint of trade," are not clearly defined.

## READING 41

1. The net earnings derived by the United States from Federal reserve banks are to be used to supplement the gold reserve held against outstanding U.S. notes, or applied to the reduction of U.S. debt.
2. Open-market operations are covered in Section 14.
3. The development of the Federal Reserve Board and a central national banking system completely transformed the nation's monetary system.

## READING 42

1. The FTC can make a complaint whenever it has reason to believe that a business is using any unfair business practices.
2. The act does not apply to banks or common carriers.
3. The act is meant to protect the public interest, not the interests of private business. Students should also present an example from the excerpt; for example, Section 5, Paragraph 2.

## READING 43

1. The president has the power to authorize the head of any governmental agency to provide foreign aid.
2. The Lend-Lease program would automatically terminate on June 30, 1943, unless both Houses of Congress passed a joint resolution stating that the program was no longer necessary to promote the defense of the United States.
3. Answers will vary but students should understand that the United States was vitally concerned with helping the Allies win the war and would not have wanted Allied countries to hesitate in seeking aid because of possible repayment difficulties.

## READING 44

1. The act applies to all federal elections.
2. The attorney general must give the board or authority notice of the complaint and certify that the board or authority has had appropriate time to correct the situation.
3. The two primary reasons for the importance of this act are that it states in no uncertain terms that *no* person shall be discriminated against—including women and all races of people; and the act includes the four fundamental social issues of voting, public accommodations, education, and employment.

## READING 45

1. The act sets no educational requirements for voting.
2. The act states that poll taxes prevent some people of limited means from voting, they do not have a legiti-

mate benefit to the state, and they often prevent people from voting because of race or color.

3. Poll taxes and testing are undemocratic because they take the political voice away from many people, thus eliminating the opportunity for lower-income and undereducated people to make fundamental social changes and improve their situations. They also extend the power of the educated and wealthy elite.

## READING 46

1. Limitations on interest rates create inequities for depositors, hinder competition among financial institutions, and do not help to provide funds for mortgage lending.
2. The goals of the committee are to phase-out and ultimately eliminate limitations on maximum interest rates and dividend payments.
3. People who had money to invest, even small amounts of money, experienced the greatest benefits from this act because financial institutions were forced to offer them competitive rates and services.

## READING 47

1. Discrimination on the basis of disability differed from discrimination based on other factors because people with disabilities had no legal means by which to address their grievances. Other people who experienced discrimination were protected by the Civil Rights Act of 1964.
2. Discrimination on the basis of disability is harmful to society as a whole because it forces people with disabilities to be dependent on government funds and services for tasks that they would be capable of completing if the opportunity were available to them.
3. Answers will vary but students should consider the accommodations made at their school for people with disabilities.

## READING 48

1. According to Locke, only when all people have relinquished their natural powers and resigned the preservation of their property to a sovereign authority can political society be achieved.
2. The absolute prince is still in the state of nature because he has not conceded to give up any of his natural powers and, therefore, answers to no common judge or standing rule.
3. Locke's theory that civil society can be achieved only when all members of society resign their natural rights and consent to the rules of the community parallels the American Declaration of Independence,

which holds that governments derive their power from the consent of the governed.

## READING 49

1. A person remains free for the following reasons: each person gives all of himself or herself and thus the condition for all people is equal and no one needs to harm or burden anyone else; since all people concede to join the contract, the common will is a perfect association and the will of all the people determines the actions of the community; and all people gain the equivalent of what they lose by joining the contract.
2. People lose an unlimited right to everything that tempts them and gain civil liberty and the right to everything they own.
3. Rousseau states that all people who enter into the social contract perceive all other members of the contract as indispensable to the whole of society. Students should also comment on the validity of this statement.

## READING 50

1. The sum of a society's capital determines the size of its industry.
2. According to Smith's theory of the invisible hand, an individual, in pursuing his own best interest, will usually prefer a domestic market and will naturally direct that market in a way that best supports the domestic industry.
3. Answers will vary but should consider the issues of free markets as well as the necessity for some government intervention to ensure the fairness of business activities.

## READING 51

1. Paine calls Europe the parent country of America because the people seeking asylum from persecution had come to America from all over Europe, not just England.
2. Paine argues that an alliance with Britain will involve America in European wars that it otherwise would not be a party to.
3. Paine's pamphlet was so successful because it appealed to the common man.

## READING 52

1. The term *faction* can be defined as a number of citizens who are united in a common interest.
2. The causes of factions cannot be removed because freedom of opinion is vital to human existence and

by destroying that freedom, you take away the fundamental basis of democracy.

3. Answers will vary but students should provide an assessment of the necessity of factions in a democratic society, as well as an example of a present-day interest group.

## READING 53

1. Hamilton states that if the president's time in office is too short, the president will not be interested enough to take any real action.

2. The length of the president's term in office relates to the legislature in the influence legislators have over their constituents to support the president's re-election.

3. Students who think that four years is too short a tenure may say that this length of time does not permit the president to put into effect all of his or her plans. Students who think that four years is sufficient may say that a longer term in office would make the president complacent and ineffective.

## READING 54

1. If the supply of Commodity A is much greater than that of Commodity B, a large quantity of Commodity A will be sold for a smaller quantity of Commodity B.

2. If the demand for a commodity is high, the supply of that commodity will be increased (assuming that the supply *can* be increased).

3. Students should provide a scenario similar to the following: There could be a freeze and most of the corn crops could be destroyed. This would cause supply to be extremely low. If the freeze did not affect the crops necessary for the production of cloth, a small amount of corn would trade for a large amount of cloth. If, however, the crops necessary for the production of cloth also were affected and the supply of cloth was also low, the amount at which they trade for each other would most likely be equal.

## READING 55

1. Nations are able to form political assemblies because nations contain large numbers of people with diverse talents and interests.

2. Towns are the strength of free nations because they bring liberty and political discussion within people's reach.

3. Answers will vary but should include an assessment of the importance of towns and cities in today's society.

## READING 56

1. Thoreau states that the American people are responsible for the success of the United States and that the government has kept the nation from achieving more.

2. Thoreau believes it is appropriate to break the law if obeying the law causes an injustice to another person.

3. Thoreau is assuming that people will break the law only to avoid injustice. For Thoreau's theory to work, people would have to be of strong moral character. Students should agree or disagree with Thoreau's assumption that people will break only those laws that they perceive as unjust and, in doing so, will not harm any other person. Students should also comment on the potential dangers to a society in which each person is the judge of his or her own actions.

## READING 57

1. Mill states that if an opinion is denied a voice, one of two things can happen: if the opinion is right, people are denied the opportunity of knowing it; and if it is wrong, people are denied the clearer view of the right opinion.

2. An opinion can be proven to be correct only if it is subjected to, and withstands, contradictory opinions.

3. Answers will vary but students should consider the repercussions both of voicing an opinion and of silencing an opinion.

## READING 58

1. A use-value is the utility of a given commodity. It is determined only by its use or consumption.

2. A commodity's use-value is determined by the quality and utility of the commodity; the exchange-value, on the other hand, is determined only by the quantity for which it is exchanged for another commodity.

3. Answers will vary but students should consider the quality and usefulness of commodities versus the quantity for which commodities may be exchanged for other commodities.

## READING 59

1. The bourgeoisie has sacrificed personal worth and numberless other fundamental freedoms in exchange for free trade.

2. For the proletariat to be free, national differences between classes of people must be abolished.

3. Answers will vary but students may mention the lack of incentive to work that accompanies a lack of economic incentive, the possibilities of corruption in a government that controls all the means of produc-

tion, and restrictions on the rights and liberties of the people.

## READING 60

1. Economic motives have more of an impact because they extend over a larger part of everyday life—for example, daily activities in the workplace, interaction with fellow workers, and so on.
2. Marshall states that economics has not attracted the world's great thinkers because such people generally are not concerned with the study of wealth.
3. Answers will vary but students should comment on whether or not they agree with the importance of economic motives on people.

## READING 61

1. Ford decided that the big money was in mass production, quick turnover, and easily interchangeable parts.
2. Ford was having trouble keeping men employed at his factory. He remedied it by paying higher wages and providing incentives to stay with the company.
3. Ford's policies would be considered discriminatory in today's workplace. He would have to hire women, and he would be unable to hire people based on their marital status or personal appearance.

## READING 62

1. People panicked and sold stocks at record levels; had they not panicked, the stocks may have risen naturally.
2. Tuesday was the most devastating day because banks could no longer prevent the losses. They had managed to ward off the financial crisis for several days, but, as people rushed to withdraw their savings, banks were forced to close because they simply did not have the capital to cover the mass amount of trading.
3. The significance of Wall Street being busy is that many people had a lot of cash because they had just sold their stocks. The booming business of Wall Street businesses demonstrates that people were attempting to cling to the economic prosperity of the previous decade, ignoring the fact that the economic infrastructure of the United States would crumble.

## READING 63

1. The employment agencies were charging men to find them jobs and then sending them to jobs for which they were not qualified. Men would thus have to come back to the agency and pay to receive another job.
2. Monroe was not offered more assistance at the institution because he was not a released prisoner and thus the state was not obligated to help him.
3. The Great Depression was emotionally devastating because hardworking Americans were forced into poverty and desperation and could find no way out of their predicament.

## READING 64

1. Consumers are price conscious because they are poor in relation to the extent of their wants and thus are constantly trying to balance their wants with their financial means of achieving them.
2. Retailers are better able to lower prices because they are more efficient, they are more knowledgeable in assessing quality, they are able to search greater possibilities for less expensive supplies, and they can purchase larger quantities from manufacturers and thus can force producers to make improvements.
3. It would probably be more economical to shop at a large chain store because they purchase greater quantities and have more sources from which to buy their goods. Thus they can offer products at lower prices to the consumer.

## READING 65

1. Statehood would provide Alaskans with the rights of U.S. citizenship, opportunity for economic development, and financial assistance for social welfare programs such as medical treatment and education.
2. Gruening notes that the immense territory and vast terrain of Alaska would be instrumental for defense and, by granting Alaska statehood, Congress would have members familiar with the territory. He also makes the argument that the Alaskan people are the type of Americans who will help the country prosper.
3. Answers will vary but students should explain why they found the argument convincing.

## READING 66

1. Senators are responsible to constituents, the good of the United States as a whole, personal conscience, and party loyalty.
2. A senator would go against local interests when the benefits to the nation as a whole outweighed the benefits to his or her constituents alone.
3. A senator's primary responsibility is to the constituents because promoting the wishes of the people is the "essence of democracy."

### READING 67

1. The two assumptions are that the urgency of wants does not diminish as more wants are satisfied, and that wants originate in the particular desires of the consumer.
2. Producers create consumer demand through advertising and salesmanship.
3. Galbraith states that emulation is a key factor in determining an individual's wants; and wants, in turn, determine demand. Students should provide an example such as the following: a friend has a new pair of a particular brand of basketball shoes, he or she emulates that friend, he or she then chooses to purchase a pair of those shoes, thus increasing consumer demand.

### READING 68

1. It is so harmful because it is irreversible.
2. The dangers of insecticides are that they destroy all insects, infect birds and fish, coat leaves with deadly film, and remain in the soil for many generations.
3. "Control of nature" refers to the arrogant notion held by humans that they should control the environment. It is harmful because as humans attempt to control nature for themselves they may destroy the natural equilibrium of the environment.

### READING 69

1. Gault was denied the rights to bail, indictment by a grand jury, public trial, and trial by jury.
2. Both the juvenile and his or her parents must be notified of the rights of the accused.
3. Fortas states that due process of law is the foundation of an individual's freedom. Answers should also comment on the importance of due process; for example, all other rights and freedoms are meaningless unless a person is guaranteed that he or she will not face arbitrary arrest and punishment.

### READING 70

1. Injustice is tolerable only if it is done to avoid a greater injustice.
2. The purposes of the principles of justice are to provide a way of assigning rights and duties to the institutions of society and to define the appropriate distribution of benefits and burdens placed on a society.
3. Rawls's theory that people with opposing conceptions of justice are able to agree is dependent on the existence of institutions that do not make arbitrary distinctions between persons; in other words, on a political system free of discrimination.

### READING 71

1. The trade volume was low because the developed countries were self-sufficient and developing countries were forced to rely only on seacoast markets because they did not have railways.
2. An industrial revolution is dependent on an agricultural revolution because the industrial sector must be able to purchase the food and raw materials necessary for industrial production and subsistence from the domestic market. It is expensive and counterproductive to export manufacturing supplies and import agricultural necessities.
3. A lack of industrialization and development is a serious problem in countries that have rapid and continued population growth. As the population increases, it becomes increasingly difficult for the country to care for its people.

### READING 72

1. The framers believed that, since the electoral vote would be indecisive, the House of Representatives—each state having one vote—would elect the president and the second-place finisher would be vice president.
2. The primary change in the party system over the 30 years is that members of Congress no longer must forge a party alliance, and people no longer have to serve in public office for many years prior to their election to Congress.
3. O'Neill states that recent changes in the political party system have been detrimental to Congress. Answers should also include a statement that agrees or disagrees with O'Neill's assessment.

### READING 73

1. The contract promises to hold congressmembers to more ethical standards, to cut the size of government, to require more disclosure of congressional business, and to change the number of members needed to pass a tax increase.
2. The contract proposes to deal with teenage pregnancy, to support per-child tax credits, to repeal the marriage tax penalty, to promote parents' involvement in their children's education, and to make an elderly dependent care tax incentive.
3. Answers will vary but students should consider the issue of disclosure of party platforms and/or the issue of political propaganda as a means of winning votes.